Also available at all good book stores

9781785315510

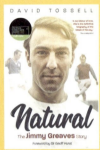

9781785314902

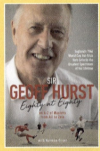

9781801501286

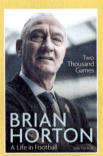

9781785316685

9781785316807

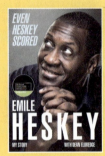

9781785315008

9781785316333

9781785316760

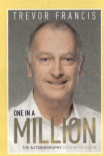

9781785314995

LOSING MY
SPURS

ANTHONY POTTS

LOSING MY
SPURS

GAZZA, THE GRIEF
AND THE GLORY

The Memoirs of a Failed Footballer

First published by Pitch Publishing, 2021

Pitch Publishing
A2 Yeoman Gate
Yeoman Way
Worthing
Sussex
BN13 3QZ
www.pitchpublishing.co.uk
info@pitchpublishing.co.uk

ISBN 978 1 80150 051 7

Typesetting and origination by Pitch Publishing
Printed and bound in India by Replika Press Pvt. Ltd.

Contents

To my wife Sonya, my family and my close friends – thank you for being there for me. Without your love and support there would be no story to tell.

Prologue

IT WAS Paul Stewart, the ex-Tottenham Hotspur and England footballer, who told me that I should write a book about my time at Spurs with Paul Gascoigne. I had just stayed overnight at the house that Gazza shared with Paul following another eventful day in Gazza's company. I thought about it, but soon dismissed the idea. I knew that to write it I would need to do it as part of my own story, and who would want to read a book about me? There are a million of me out there: someone who chased their dream but never quite made it. I'm too normal.

Then a few things happened.

First of all, I wrote a book. I had always wanted to, I had the idea for years, but I finally put pen to paper. Although by the time I wrote it, it was finger to keyboard. It was based on my experiences at Spurs through the eyes of a fictional teenager called Liam Osborne, and on the whole, it was well received. I enjoyed the process, so I wrote another one. This too did okay. I found that I enjoyed writing. Next, I started to write a regular blog, and people seemed to enjoy it and liked some of the things I had to say.

Then Jeremy Wisten, a youth team player at Manchester City, committed suicide after being released from the club having been there since the age of 13. It resonated with me. I wrote a blog about how tough it is having your dreams wrenched away from you at a young age. I was shocked at how many people got in touch and said that they'd had the same low points, the same negative experiences. It made me think that it was an issue that needed to be put into a wider forum.

Lastly, I had people tell me that my books about the fictional Liam Osborne had helped their children in dealing with the harsher side of football. The fact that Liam didn't give up had shown their children that if you want something enough then you have to fight for it, and told them they weren't the only ones going through what they were going through.

In the end, I decided that my normalness was exactly why I could and *should* write this book. Sometimes it's not the millionaire success stories that matter the most.

I have tried to be honest. I have never really spoken about a lot of the events in this book, and I actually feel better having written some of them down. I am sure a lot of people who know me will be surprised by some of what they read as I can be quite a private person. I have always fought against being the bloke in the pub who would have been a player 'if only'.

1

Jumpers for Goalposts

'POTTSY, IT'S my knee. It's f***ed. I saw the X-ray, they're saying it's nothing but I'm telling you it's f***ed.'

'What do you want to do?' I asked.

'We need to get back to London, get John to look at it. I'll get Jimmy to drive us.'

This conversation took place in the early hours of 29 September 1991. I was standing, more like swaying, in a quiet corner of the Newcastle Freeman Hospital. I had been drinking for two days and was talking to a very distressed Paul Gascoigne, arguably the most talented player in English history.

This wasn't how I had pictured life as a professional footballer.

* * *

I can't remember a time when I wasn't obsessed by football. As I have got older, I have managed this obsession but it is still there.

I'm not one of those who has incredibly early memories and can't recall living in the womb or being held as a baby. Before the age of about four is a complete mystery to me, but I can remember Arsenal getting to three consecutive FA Cup finals at the end of the 1970s. I was five for the first, against Ipswich Town. This was in a time when the FA Cup was the pinnacle of the footballing calendar. I can remember the excitement of the build-up during the week. The day itself was a real event. It was shown all day on ITV and BBC and I would watch every minute, flicking backwards and forwards from channel to channel to find the best segments. Meet the players, how they got there, the fitting of the cup final suit, the FA Cup song and joining the players as they left the hotel to go to the game. I loved it all. I would get some sweets and sit down on the floor of the living room with my dad and watch five hours of build-up followed by the game itself. I would physically shake with excitement.

My dad, Michael, takes his football very seriously. He has never hidden his annoyance if his concentration on the game is interrupted, and everyone in our house knew not to make a noise when the football was on. I know I used to irritate him with my inane questions. I used to try so hard to sit there in silence, but my excitement always got the better of me. Seven hours is a long time for any child to be quiet and I'm sure my dad was relieved when we finally got a second television and I could watch the build-up in a different room. I would still go back for the game itself, though.

Years later, I used to watch *Match of the Day* with my dad. It was the only programme I was allowed to stay up past my bedtime for. He would spend all evening avoiding the results as he didn't want to know the scores before he watched the highlights. The radio in the car would be switched off, and he would avoid anyone who might tell him the score. When it came to the time that *Match of the Day* was due to start, he would turn the television on and off, really quickly, in case the news had overrun, as at the end of the bulletins they gave the football scores. If it overran, and he saw the results flash up on the screen, the air would turn blue. My mum, Patricia, would then usher me out of the room; it was a similar thing when he was doing DIY and it wasn't going as smoothly as he had anticipated. I would be transferred to the garden before I heard some words that my young ears weren't yet ready for.

My dad was a latecomer to football. It was always a regret for him that as a young man, in 1963, he and my mum had owned a flat that overlooked Highbury, the home of Arsenal. He had a perfect view of the action, which Arsenal fans would have killed for. But, at that time, he had no interest in watching the game, and would even make a point of leaving the flat on a Saturday afternoon as the noise of the crowd would disturb his day. He played football as a young man but never watched it and was never really a fan. The World Cup in 1966 was the event that ignited his love for football. He then began watching Millwall with my mum's dad and ended up being a season ticket holder. He actually missed the birth of my sister while queuing to get a season ticket for Millwall in 1968, something my nan never let him forget. He was lucky that the team he watched ended up evolving into the class of 1971, thought by most Millwall fans to be their best ever. Millwall were always my second team growing up. They started an obsession for football with my dad which he then passed on to me.

When I was just three years old, my dad was involved in a motorbike accident which left him in Greenwich Hospital for nearly three years. I was five when he eventually left. It was a bad break to his leg, which got infected, and they spent all that time trying to save the limb. The ward he was on was full of patients in similar situations. Eventually, they had to concede that they could not save it.

My mum used to regularly take me and my sister Sarah to visit my dad at the hospital. After they heard the news that my dad's leg was to be amputated, my mum took me aside before a visit to the hospital and explained what was going to happen. They were very worried about how I might react with me still being so young. *The Six Million Dollar Man* was a very popular programme at the time, and my dad's new leg was sold to me as a bionic one, just like Colonel Steve Austin. The thought was that rather than me seeing the amputation as a disability, it would convince me that it was actually a good thing. Far from being bothered by it, I was envious. For years I thought my dad could leap giant buildings in a single bound. He must have got sick of me constantly asking him questions about his 'bionic' leg. My dad said that on that particular visit he was sitting in his bed waiting for us when a very loud voice could be heard from the corridor shouting excitedly, 'Daddy, they're cutting off your leg today!'

The way my dad tells it, everyone in the ward turned to stare at the door in horror, praying it wasn't going to be their kid who walked in the door. The group sigh of relief could be heard in the hospital car park.

When my dad was in the hospital, he became friends with a patient in the next bed to him, who had two broken legs. It turned out that he was a safe breaker who had been breaking into an office when he fell through the roof. His accomplices had to carry him back out and drive him home in agony. They then set it up at his house to make it look like he had fallen off a ladder. He was well known to the police and they knew he had been the one who had fallen through the roof but they had no evidence so couldn't charge him. In conversation, he told my dad of a big job they had planned. From my knowledge of cop shows, I think you would call it a 'blag'. He asked my dad if he would want to be the getaway driver. My dad said yes! He figured that he wasn't known to the police so no one would suspect him. In the end, the amputation meant he couldn't take part.

I still don't know if the 'blag' was a success.

My dad would often tell us stories of some of the things he got up to as a young man, normally with my mum trying to shush him as she didn't think it was the best example to set. I guess you would call him 'old school'. He always had an angle on every job he did and, as a young man, if he had enough money for a nice suit and to be able to get drunk at the weekend, he was content. When I was a child, he was very strict and instilled in me good manners and respect. I was always very conscious of not wanting to upset or disappoint him. He is very big on family, and some of my fondest memories of my childhood are holidays in a caravan at various places around England.

After the accident he was unable to do a job of his choice, having to take the first job that was available. His options were limited. This was before everything was so politically correct and if you went for a job interview, having one leg put you in a worse position than someone with two. As a result, he worked for nearly 20 years for British Telecom, doing a job he hated. He did it purely to provide for his family. He was a proud man and to not work and earn his own money was never an option. He hated it but he would have done his job to the best of his ability; he has always been a perfectionist. He also would not have done an additional second of work than he had to. If management asked him to do something that he felt wasn't part of his job, then he would have refused to do it. It was a job to him and if it wasn't in his job description then he wasn't doing it. He saw his sick leave entitlement as days due off that he would always take every second of. I can remember him planning out when he was going to take them at the start of each working year. I was always aware of the sacrifices that he had to make to build a future for his family.

Apparently after the operation, when he was given the all clear to go home, they were still very worried about how I might react. These worries soon disappeared when, on his first attempt to get up the stairs on one leg, I sprinted through the gap where his leg used to be, to beat him to the top.

I don't remember much of him being at the hospital, but I can only imagine how difficult it must have been for both him and my mum. My dad was in constant pain, and has been ever since, and he was stuck in a hospital bed while my mum struggled to bring up two young children alone. She really held our family together at this time and she was always on the go. My sister, Sarah, is four years older than me and was already at primary school, but I was still too young for school. I can remember that my mum used to clean houses for extra money, and she would have to bring me along as she couldn't afford childcare. It must have taken her twice as long having to clean up after me as well as do the job she was paid for. It sounds like a cliché but both my parents have always been sources of inspiration to me for how they have dealt with my dad's disability. He is in almost constant pain and has been for more than 40 years due to complications with the amputation. Yet when I look back on my childhood it was blissful, I never felt like I missed out on anything or that it was any different to anybody else's. That's a credit to both my parents.

I was born and lived in Welling, in south-east London. Charlton Athletic were my local side but this was not a good time in their history, as they had low attendances and struggled financially. Growing up, everyone I knew was an Arsenal fan. I say everyone; there was one kid down my street who supported Nottingham Forest. He was always in their kit. It is incredible to think that they won back-to-back European Cups in 1979 and 1980. At the time, supporting Forest in Welling was the equivalent of a Londoner supporting Manchester City or Manchester United: a glory hunter or plastic fan, as they are now called. Unfortunately for him the glory didn't last long, but credit to him, he still supports them even now.

The kids who played out in the street in my road were all dressed in replica Arsenal kits and I became a fully fledged fan when I was given a hand-me-down strip from a boy on my street called Alan. I was only about five and it was far too big for me. I had to roll the sleeves up about eight times just to be able to use my hands and a strong gust of wind would have seen me take flight like Mary Poppins. So that was me, five years old and an Arsenal fan whether I liked it or not. I loved that top and still have it even now. The funny thing is that it was the kit from when Arsenal did the double in 1971, which was a year before I was born, so it was already six years out of date when I got it.

I consider myself to be fortunate as being the last generation that really properly played outside. They call us Generation X. There was one reason that we played out so much; there was literally nothing else to do. There were only three TV channels, and no internet or video games. Children's TV lasted about an hour and a half and most of that was educational, with programmes like *Why Don't You?*, *John Craven's Newsround* or *Blue Peter*. I had just spent my day having to learn things at school and didn't want to do it in my free time too. Every night I would race home from school to watch cartoons or *Grange Hill* before having my tea, then go out playing football until the street lights came on. Playing out, running around, making up games, laughing and having fun with your mates. It genuinely doesn't get any better than that. The street lights were my signal that it was late and I had to come in; there were no mobile phones then. The older children would play out under the lights until their parents screamed their name from the doorsteps of their houses.

We would use the kerbs as touchlines and the tar lines across the road as the goal line. There were hardly any cars and most were on driveways. Occasionally a shout of 'Car!' would go up and we would grab the ball and wait on the pavement for it to go past. What few cars were parked on the road – no household had more than one car – were like magnets to the ball. It always seemed to get stuck underneath them. Then it would be the job of the kid with the longest legs to lay on the floor and try and scoop the ball back out from underneath. Many a pair of trousers were ruined by oil from under the car.

The footballs we played with cost about a pound and would often burst and then we would all club together enough money to buy a new one from the corner shop. They were air floaters and almost impossible to control as they were so light and flimsy. If you owned the ball, you literally owned the game; everyone was too scared that you would take your ball and go home. These matches were often rough and bad-tempered and there were always fights but these would be instantly forgotten and forgiven.

The neighbours were our biggest problem. The ball would end up in gardens, and we all knew which gardens we were okay to go in and which ones we had to sneak into. The rule was if you kicked it in the garden, then you had to get it. At this time, you knew the names of all your neighbours and I can remember hating or liking them all based on how annoyed they got if our ball went in their garden. The best tactic was to get in and out as quickly as possible before you were spotted. Being shouted at and threatened by neighbours was a regular occurrence, unlike today where people are too scared of repercussions. All the people in my street knew who I was and where I lived and they would be around my house in a heartbeat if I got too lippy or the ball went into a garden too many times. Then the doorstep shout would come, and you would make the walk of shame, banished indoors with a smack round the back of your legs for damaging a plant or not showing respect to your elders. It was a relief when the summer came and we could go and play on the heath at the top of the road.

Bostall Heath was where I really learned my football. In the summer, I would play until it was too dark to see the ball. We would take spare clothes to put down as goalposts and put them in front of the biggest bush on the edge of the heath so that we wouldn't have to keep running after the ball if the keeper didn't save it. It did mean we would be scratched to pieces trying to recover the ball. I didn't have many friends outside of school my own age; you played with the kids who lived near you and the children in my street were all three or four years older than me. It certainly helped my football development. On the heath there used to be huge games sometimes with as many as 30 or 40 kids. I was still about seven or eight while most of the players were teenagers. I was by far the smallest but would often get picked quite early as I wouldn't stop running and was always comfortable with a ball at my feet. I used to love it when they said good things about my footballing skills and I was always trying to impress them.

It is easy to look back on this time with rose-tinted glasses, but half the reason we were allowed out so much was because of an ignorance to the dangers and the lack of cars. Every park had a strange adult who you knew to stay clear of and most families had a peculiar uncle who you were told to stay away from too. There was a lack of real awareness of the dangers – even my 'friends' I was playing football with on the heath. It was only later that I realised that these kids were all truanting from school. I would race home from primary school and go straight up the heath in the summer, often forgoing my tea until later. These kids, who were supposed to be at the local comprehensive school, known locally as Elsa, would already be there smoking, drinking and doing drugs. But I didn't care, I was there to play football. Besides, I had no reference point, I just thought it was normal. They would offer me cigarettes and swigs of their drink, but I wasn't interested. Footballers didn't drink or smoke (or so I thought) so neither would I! As dodgy as they were, they all looked after me and I never felt threatened in any way. I was by far the youngest and they were very protective towards me. If we didn't have a ball to play with, they would ask me if any footballs had gone up on my primary school roof during break time that day. If any had, they would scale the gate, climb on the roof and take the ball to continue the game.

There was a serious gang problem on the estate near my house, and I can remember that huge fights and stabbings were not unusual. One time, a kid got stabbed in an alleyway next to my school as I walked through it and a couple of the kids from the heath, who were involved in the incident, practically picked me up and ran me away from the trouble. Arson was another big problem; schools were regularly burnt down and fires were always being set in the woods next to the heath. Racism was also rife. The National Front had their offices in Welling and used to give out leaflets outside the local schools. The local council cleaners would get beaten up for trying to take these posters down. Racist graffiti was everywhere. It was based largely on a fear of the unknown. In 13 years of education based around Welling I can count the number of class-mates who weren't white British on one hand, and yet this was real hate. In 1977 there was a riot in Lewisham, our neighbouring borough, after a National Front march. It had the dubious distinction of being the first use of riot shields in mainland England. People have short memories when they talk about the kids of today.

My regular football partner in crime at this age was a kid called Nicky Georgiou. He was four years older than me and had been in my sister's class in Hillsgrove, our local primary school. He was incredibly skilful, and I was always trying to emulate what he did. He went to Elsa, which was the same school the kids from the heath were supposed to be at. Elsa had an awful reputation in the area, and these kids were the worst of a bad lot. Nicky wasn't as keen as me to join in their games on the heath because he was more aware of what they were really like. If you saw these kids walking down the road towards you, you would turn around and walk the other way. One of them used to threaten Nicky to make him join in the matches and, in the end, Nicky had to tell a teacher at his school and they put the equivalent of a restraining order on this kid. I just carried on blissfully unaware, happy that there was always a game of football to play in.

2

Woolies Wonders

I JOINED my first football team at the age of eight. It was pure luck that I joined such a strong group. Villacourt Rovers was a local club that had sides from under-ten all the way to adults. Their under-ten side had some talented young players but the league had said they were too young to play at that age. As a result, Villacourt formed a brand-new under-nine team called Villa. One of the local kids, Paul Rooke, who was himself a decent footballer, had seen me playing in the street and recommended me. It meant that I had to get my first pair of football boots. I was so excited. They were from Woolworths and were called Winfields, although they were locally known as Woolies Wonders. They were awful; they had three stripes like Adidas, but that was where the similarity ended. They had a harsh feel to them because they were made of a hard, unbending plastic. I remember trying them out on the heath a couple of days before my first game and I could barely walk in them, let alone run. When I got home my feet were one big blister. In the end, I played my very first football match in trainers as I couldn't even get the boots back on to my feet.

The game itself was fantastic; wearing a proper kit, having a team talk and eating half-time oranges. The only problem was that I played at centre-half and hated it there. I just wanted to score goals and found it boring playing at the back, but won so I started the next game there too, which was another victory. I can still remember being green with envy as we left the pitch seeing my team-mates celebrating their goals. One kid in particular scored about five in my first game. I wanted some of that. I wanted to score goals. The manager saw me sulking at the end of the game and asked what was wrong so I told him, 'I want to play up front like Kenny Dalglish!'

In the next game I played up front, and I scored a couple of goals. I never played anywhere else for them again. It was an incredible team and we went unbeaten, including friendlies, for nearly five years. Not just unbeaten but we *won* every game, the majority by five or more goals. It was like a snowball; the better we did the more players wanted to join us and the better we got. We won the London Cup three years on the spin so they wouldn't let us enter it. When they let us back in, we won it again. Arsenal asked if we could be their youth team, but our manager refused and said that he wanted our players to be signed on their own individual merit. And we did. Everyone, even our substitutes, were on the books of a professional team. About seven of us were signed by Charlton and, although there were no games to play at the time, we got to train on AstroTurf, when it still felt like something special.

Just a point on the facilities at this time. Villacourt Rovers had a privately owned sports ground in Blackheath at the end of a private road. It was fantastic. The pitches and changing rooms were pristine. But we were the exception, and some of the pitches we played on would not be allowed these days – they were so uneven they were ankle breakers. Games were never called off. Often there would be hardly any grass, and even if there was any it would be almost up to your knees in places. I can even recall playing on some pitches with trees on them where the touchline curved around the tree.

Then there was training. You trained in school halls on concrete floors or on school playgrounds in the dark. If you were lucky enough to have this new-fangled AstroTurf that had just started popping up, you were basically playing on a thin carpet laid over concrete. You might as well have painted the concrete green. Injuries were commonplace and you just played through most of them. I played the majority of matches with knee supports or ankle supports, but I didn't care, and no one seemed bothered.

In those five years I lived the equivalent of a footballing utopia. I was never a substitute or substituted on any team I played for and scored in almost every game I played. I was scoring well over 100 goals every year. I got in my school team a year early, made the district side (Bexley) and the county side (Kent). Our district and county teams would also sweep all before them, as seven of the players came from Villacourt. We were all in the starting 11 and it felt just like playing for Villacourt but with a different kit. It would have been the whole team, but some lived in a different county so played for Inner London.

I would play midweek for my school, train with Charlton twice a week and Villacourt once a week. Then when I wasn't playing or training, I would be on the heath playing football. If no one was about then I would spend hours in the street doing keep-ups and practising tricks. On a Saturday morning I would play for my district, county or school. On a Saturday afternoon, I would go and watch football with my dad and on Sunday I would play for Villacourt. Yet I can never remember being coached. I can never remember someone helping me with my game, although I can't remember someone having a go at me for doing the wrong thing either. No one told me how to play football. I learned by playing; I learned by failing. If I dribbled when I should have passed, then I would learn because I would lose the ball.

At that age, I just played because I loved playing. I think players now are over-coached. I was always allowed to do my own thing when I played. If I wanted to shoot, I shot. If I wanted to dribble then I dribbled. The easy option isn't always the best option. Why limit young players? There is plenty of time to coach and discipline them. I guess it helped that we were winning and I was playing well, so no one could say too much anyway.

3

Football Existed Before 1992

MY DAD started to take me to football matches when I was about eight or nine, at the start of the 1980s. The Nottingham Forest supporter down my street, David Wagner, was a huge football fan but his dad wasn't. So, at first, my dad used to take him. It was just non-league. They mainly watched Welling United, but if they weren't at home, they watched Dartford, Gravesend and Northfleet or Erith and Belvedere. All four teams were decent and played a level or two below the Football League. You might think I was envious of David, but I didn't care. I was happy just playing and wasn't too interested in watching live matches. I used to travel in the car when my mum dropped them both off, and then travel down again to pick them up.

In between I would be on the heath playing football; often I would have to sit on a towel in the back of the car as I was still caked in mud from playing.

I remember my dad trying me out at an Erith and Belvedere game when I was about seven. I spent the whole match climbing over the terraces and barely looked at the pitch. It was clear I wasn't ready. Then Welling started to get together a good team and the crowds got a little bigger. When me and my mum picked Dad and David up, we would sometimes be early and I could hear the crowd from the car. In the end I asked if I could come along too. Of course, the answer was yes, so from that point on every Saturday afternoon would be spent watching football.

My dad always said it was a good education for me as you could get up close to the players and see everything properly, even hear them shouting and swearing at each other. The football was fast, furious and physical. There were often sendings off and the odd fight. But there were also some very good players. In that Welling team were Andy Townsend and Tony Agana, who would both go on to play at the highest level. Andy was my favourite player. Even at that age he was clearly too good for that level. He scored some spectacular goals that first year I watched, and I used to spend most of the match just following him.

Thankfully non-league football hasn't changed much, and the experience you get now would be much the same, except more expensive! It was next to nothing to watch a game of football back then, even at professional levels. Now, entry, a pie, a drink and a programme would set you back about £10 to £20 at non-league. If you have a couple of kids, that's a lot of money to be shelling out every weekend.

The change in league football is even worse. As my football progressed my dad started taking me to Millwall to see better players. I know what you're thinking, Millwall? Better players? But they had a decent side, they were managed by George Graham and went one season unbeaten at home and won promotion to the Second Division. Many of that team were still there when they gained promotion to the First Division, and included a very young Teddy Sheringham and John Fashanu. I used to love going to The Den, although if I am honest, I spent a lot of the time watching the crowd. There was often violence and it could get quite scary. I never felt threatened, though, and actually quite enjoyed watching the trouble. As an adult I now view it differently, but as a kid it just seemed exciting.

It was around this time that our Villacourt manager, Barry Owen, used to take a group of us to watch Arsenal play. He drove a taxi so there would be about five or six of us in the back of his cab. I was star-struck. Seeing my heroes up close was incredible. Players like Tony Woodcock and Kenny Sansom. It wasn't a great Arsenal side but I didn't care. I would spend the game with eyes as wide as saucepans. At Highbury you used to be able to get really close to the action and one of my weird memories is us all being stunned at the size of Kenny Sansom's calves. He played left-back and when he used to take throw-ins his legs were at our eyeline and we would all look at each other like they were some sort of eighth wonder of the world. It was so easy to watch football at this time. You just turned up and paid at the turnstile; no need to book a ticket months in advance like you do now.

Unfortunately, league football has now become inaccessible to many working-class families. Ticket prices start at about £30, so for a family it costs over £100 just to get in the stadium. Add on something to eat and drink and getting to the game in the first place and you are past the budget of the average family. As a result, supporting a club feels less tribal than it used to. It used to feel like the crowd were all local to the club and lived and breathed for their football. We were never flush for money, but I can remember my dad taking me to every league ground in London one season. I can also remember watching Arsenal at Highbury, West Ham at the Boleyn Ground and Chelsea at Stamford Bridge all in one day. If you did that now you would need to remortgage.

Nowadays, the footballers are fitter and more professional, and their technical ability is higher. But football back then was better! Tackling was allowed, which meant there were fewer free kicks and the games had a better flow with fewer stoppages. As a fan, you could identify with the players. You actually believed that they cared as much as you did. The modern player is very media aware and they seem bland in comparison. The players back then had personalities. Every team seemed to have a maverick, someone who entertained and a hard man who went to war for his team. These players were always fan favourites. The maverick was always given more leeway than the other players. No one cared that they often looked a bit lazy, they loved them for special, unexpected moments that they could produce. Gazza may have been the last of these.

Then there were the terraces. It was tribal. It's true that you were crammed in standing side by side with your fellow fans, but it felt like you belonged to something bigger. Even the discomfort brought you closer. It was raw. It used to stink of urine as people relieved themselves at the back of the stands, unless you were at West Ham where it was other people's pockets that they used. The singing was constant and the abuse horrific. There was also real humour, with hilarious things shouted out that would bring a roar of laughter. The language was crass and raw. To a ten-year-old boy it was incredible, better than Disneyland. That atmosphere can never be replicated.

Quite rightly, terracing has long gone. Even back then when a goal was scored or a chance created the crowd would surge forward, literally carrying you with it. Then you would be crushed against the concrete barrier until everyone returned to their regular spot. Hillsborough was an accident in waiting for years. Many times, my dad would brace himself to protect me and my mum from the surging fans. That's right, my mum. Once my sister was old enough to be left alone, my mum graduated from chauffeur to a regular football fan and she is actually quite knowledgeable about football. My sister has no interest in football and never did, but she was a very good dancer and my mum had to ferry her around to competitions and practice as well as me to my football. Thinking back, I don't know how she managed it, but there are still parents up and down the country sacrificing themselves to give their children the best possible childhood. For five years, my mum watched pretty much every game I played; I honestly can't remember her missing one, although I am sure she must have.

Finally, when I hit 13, she sat me down and told me that I was old enough to get myself to football. She said she would still buy my boots but everything else was down to me. It felt good to be considered grown up, but it was a sad day on reflection. After my matches, in the car on the way home, my mum would always tell me if she thought I played well or not. She was very honest but didn't really care and wasn't judgemental. If I scored, she would buy me a packet of salt and vinegar crisps for the journey home. But there were never any recriminations if I played badly. There was something special about eating those crisps in the back of our car. Some of my team-mates used to be scared to go back home after a bad performance knowing the abuse they would get off their dads. Sometimes they would come back with me and we would go play football up the heath until they felt it was safe to go back home.

But me, I was in heaven; I was spending all week playing football with my friends and I felt like I was as good as anyone. I was convinced that I was going to be a professional footballer, and at this point I genuinely wanted to be the best in the world.

I know that sounds big-headed but my rationale was that someone had to be. I also thought if I didn't try then I definitely wouldn't be so what was the problem with aiming high!

I was completely single-minded. I saw everyone as my competition. If I heard someone being given praise, I would panic that they were better than me and push myself even more. In our team our best player was Kevin Horlock. He was the lad who had scored five goals in my first competitive game and had been playing a year above himself for Villacourt before our team had been started. He was a great kid, full of confidence and great to be around, but I was so jealous. I wanted people to talk about me like they spoke about him. Everyone was sure he was going to be a professional footballer. He played central midfield and scored nearly as many goals as me, but he was great in the air, a good tackler and had the sweetest left foot. In my head, I was sure I was as good as him, but I wanted everyone else to think the same as me! My parents soon twigged on to it.

'Anthony, time for bed,' my mum would say.

'Aah Mum, five more minutes, it's only 9pm.'

'Kevin goes to bed at 8.30pm,' would come the reply.

My new bedtime was now 8.30pm and I was the one enforcing it.

Those of you who are football fans, and if you are reading this then you probably are, will no doubt recognise Kevin's name. He had a great career playing for Manchester City and

West Ham United among others in a career spanning nearly 500 games. I also found out from him years later that his bed-time was a lot later than 8.30pm.

4

All Latin to Me

EVERY PART of my life was now governed by football. At school, every story I wrote was about football; every book I read was about football; every conversation I had was about football. I had four magazines delivered every week: *Match*, *Shoot!*, *Roy of the Rovers* and *Beano*. I only wanted *Beano* because there was a cartoon called 'Ball Boy', about a five-a-side football team. There was a time I could name any player in the whole Football League and I could tell you who they played for, who they used to play for and their average rating in *Match*'s weekly match reports.

By nature, I was a shy, introverted boy. I hated meeting new people and could be very self-conscious about how I looked. My ability at football helped me make friends and gave me confidence. Everyone knew me. At the age of 11, I started at Bexley Grammar School having passed my 11-plus. I wasn't too bothered about schoolwork, but I was pleased to pass just so I didn't have to go to Elsa, at this point now called Welling School. I now had more of an awareness of the children I had been hanging around with on the heath, and was worried what might happen to me if I went there. I had heard terrible stories of bog washing and the like. Bog washing was where they held your head under in a dirty toilet and flushed the chain.

I was relieved to go to the grammar school, but I hated the idea of being a grammar school child. In my head, they were all posh and snooty. I think this must have been based purely on *Beano*. I used to take off my tie and blazer on my journey to and from school in case people saw me and wanted to beat me up for being a grammar school kid! When I got in the county team I used to wear their tie and sewed their badge over my school one so that no one knew which school I went to. I used to get in trouble for it but I didn't care.

The school was actually okay, if a bit out of date. The boys were called by their last name and the girls were called by their first names. Imagine that happening now. Latin was also part of the curriculum. There were times when I would wonder what I was doing there. Sometimes in a lesson our teacher would forget to set us homework and I would be desperately trying to pack away and get out before they remembered. There would always be one child who would remind the teacher. I would be fuming, but the majority of my class would be pleased to be getting the homework. I remember a new kid starting in my class who had joined because they didn't set enough homework at his last school. His first day, I sat there looking at him like he was from another planet.

I clearly wasn't the only one who read *Beano*. On at least four occasions in my time at Bexley, other schools came down wanting to beat up anyone from the local grammar school. On two occasions the police even had to be called. Once, we were playing football on the field when concrete blocks, lumps of wood and bottles came raining down from the other side of the fence. We all had to run back into the main building. It was like an away day at Galatasaray. We weren't allowed to leave the school until the police turned up, and my blazer and tie were off before I even left the school gates that day.

I can remember my first day at my secondary school. We were all called into a big hall before being sent off to our homerooms. I hate meeting new people, my shyness really kicks in, and there I was with 120 of them, all at the same time. I took a seat near the front and kept my head down, trying not to make eye contact with anyone. I could see children already starting to make friends. They amazed me. How can you just go up to a complete stranger and start talking? It was excruciating for me. Then we were off to our homerooms; a quick scan found a seat towards the back, by the window away from everyone. I was dreading our new teacher making us stand up and introduce ourselves, or worse, talk about ourselves. It is a dread I still carry with me now if I start a new job or have to go on a course. I was kind of relieved to see a couple of children from Hillsgrove in my form room, David Foreman and Keilly Stevenson, but they were already talking to other children so I tried to stay in the background. I managed to get through to break without drawing attention to myself, but I was already feeling isolated. As shy as I was, this wasn't what I really wanted. I wished I could be like some of the other children; loud, brash and confident. I just couldn't bring myself to make the first step.

Break time was even worse as now there were nearly a thousand children. As I wandered around trying to take everything in, I stumbled upon a game of football. Some of the new year ones had been challenged by the year two children. Back then you finished primary school in year four then started at year one again in secondary. Blazers were thrown down for goalposts and I watched, desperate to play. Then I was recognised by one of the other first-years.

'You're Pottsy from Villacourt aren't you? We played against you in the cup. You can play for us.'

And that was it, ice broken, no more nerves. Once again football had stepped in and given me the push I needed. Then my football did the talking. A few nice dribbles, some nice touches, a few goals; now everyone wanted to talk to me.

Despite my misgivings, I loved my time at Bexley Grammar. I saw it like more of a social thing than educational and spent most of my time just mucking about. Breaks and lunch were different. I would practically run out of lessons so that I would have more time to play football. There was a small group of us who used to play. My best friend was a kid called Keighley Peters who was a couple of years older than me. I had met him on Bostal Heath and we used to go up there every spare second and play football. Coincidentally, he was already at Bexley Grammar so, when I started, we used to play football at every break. There was also a lad called Paul Braddick, who was in my year and would play every break time. He loved his football and would never stop running. He was the same in matches, so I used to like playing in midfield with him as he would do all my running for me. He was never shy of pointing that out to me.

Then, when I started year two, Mathew Rose moved to the school. He was an outstanding player. Even though he was a year younger he joined in with our little group every break. As a footballer, he had everything, and when he was in year three Arsenal offered him a ten-year contract. He turned it down but did sign for them when he left school. In the end he played five first-team games for Arsenal. I was so jealous. It had to be my team, didn't it! But I was genuinely happy for him at the same time, as he was the nicest kid you could ever meet; he even took his school work seriously. He was completely dedicated to his football and had the perfect temperament, and later in his career he ended up playing nearly 300 games for Queens Park Rangers. With Bexley being a grammar school, there were not many successful players to come through there. Before I joined, there was only Gavin Peacock who had ever made it to be a professional. Now there was two in two years.

Dedicating yourself to becoming a footballer as a secondary student is a sacrifice and you have to be single-minded. I played football at breaks because I loved to play, but also because it was another chance to practise. It did mean I didn't hang around with my other friends at break, and missed out on mixing with the other girls in my year, some of whom I was now showing more than a bit of interest in. It was the same outside of school. I had gravitated towards the naughtier kids at the school. There was a certain amount of rebelling against being a grammar school kid, and I could identify with that. I had more in common with them. A big group of us used to walk back from school together and we somehow turned a 25-minute walk into an hour and a half most nights as we larked around. Again though, I was playing football every night and most weekends so I never got to hang out with them too much outside of school.

I was very aware that I was missing out on a lot of the fun parts of being a teenager, but I knew what I wanted in life. It was that end goal that kept me disciplined. It meant that while they were going out, drinking, smoking, taking drugs and chasing girls, I was normally tucked up in bed after another evening training session. It is a tough thing to do, to keep turning down invitations; you have to be so focused. It makes things even worse if your career doesn't go to plan as you become acutely aware of what you missed out on.

If I had my time again, I am not sure I would make the same choices. I don't have many friends now from when I was at school. They are people I still consider as my friends but I have lost touch with a lot of them. In fact, without Facebook I would know little about them at all. Choosing to dedicate yourself to an end goal dictates that you don't have enough time to really get close to people. In the end the invitations stop, as they can only be told no so many times. Most of the friends I spent the most time with were from the teams I played in. I saw them far more than my friends at school. The problem with that is that people change teams and you often don't keep in touch. It is a football thing; they were your team-mates and now they are the opposition. You are still friendly but now you have new colleagues.

It is around this time that a lot of very good players fall by the wayside. We all know someone who was the next big thing at 13 but just drifted away from football. Danny Wareham was my best example. At 13 he was incredible. He had the choice of every professional club in the country. Southampton were desperate to sign him; they were actually keen on signing a lot of our players. They sent Danny Wallace, their best player at the time, down for Danny's birthday and were forever buying him gifts. One time they took him to a garage and when they opened it up it was full of footballing memorabilia and he was told to take what he wanted. Danny was obsessed by the Brazilian team so Southampton gave him a signed shirt. In the end he got caught up in living a normal teenage life. He was drinking, smoking, chasing girls and probably a lot more besides. Eventually he drifted out of football having done his

YTS at Charlton. I know for a fact that he remains close to his friends from school even now, and very few footballers can say the same. Knowing Danny, I'm not sure he would have any regrets, although you can never be sure.

Our goalkeeper, Lee Clarke, was also chased by Southampton at this time. He was very good in goal but also equally good out on the pitch. Southampton used the fact that Peter Shilton was their goalkeeper to tempt Lee to join them. They would get him to train with Shilton and gave him a signed photo. Lee would have been an ideal modern keeper as he was so good with his feet. The back-pass rule would not have fazed him at all and he had all the abilities you need to be an excellent goalkeeper. Unfortunately, he was tragically taken from us at the age of 19 by leukaemia.

In my second year at Bexley Grammar, I was scouted by West Ham and left Charlton to go and play for them. My football was still ticking along perfectly at this stage and everyone I knew was expecting me to become a professional, me included. I had been at Charlton since I was about eight as most of Villacourt started to train with them at that time. West Ham were known as the 'academy of football' and still had a reputation for bringing through homegrown players into their first team. More importantly, they were in the First Division, and that suited my ego.

Villacourt had now become St George's thanks to a new sponsor; it also meant a change of venue to Eltham as our new sponsor owned his own ground. A couple of the St George's players had already been scouted by Arsenal, so I was envious and starting to feel like Charlton were not a big enough club for my lofty ambitions. I felt like these players were now ahead of me and I didn't like it. Especially with it being Arsenal, my club.

Joining West Ham felt like a step up. The scout who spotted me was brilliant. Micky Dove, I think his name was. He used to get me tickets for West Ham matches and take me and a few of the other players there. He would take us down to the changing rooms and introduce us to the players and manager. I can particularly remember seeing Jan Mølby in the tunnel before West Ham played Liverpool and it was like an eclipse. He was huge. Then he went out and bossed the game in an incredible performance. All Micky Dove's efforts made me feel special, and I couldn't wait to sign. I was now 12, nearly 13, and if I had known then what was to follow I would have stayed exactly where I was.

I had built my whole world around football, and when it came tumbling down, I tumbled with it.

5

House of Cards

WHEN I look back, I don't think West Ham were ever interested in me. Three St George's players joined them that year: me, Kevin Horlock and Darren Hancock. I've told you about Kevin and at this time he was still one of the best players around. Darren, though, was something else. He had a larger-than-life personality. He would walk into a room of strangers and immediately be the centre of everything. He was the quickest and strongest player I had seen at my age. He could throw the ball from the halfway line into the goal without bouncing and had a kick like a mule. He was my best friend at Villacourt, and we also played in the same county and district sides.

There wasn't a professional club in the country that wouldn't have snapped him up, but he was joining West Ham because he was a West Ham supporter. I wonder now if they took me on as they knew I was a friend of Darren.

To be fair, it wasn't all the coaches. There was one called Jimmy Frith. Everyone at West Ham during this time would have fond memories of him. He was a great coach, and always smiling and laughing. He was the only person who took the time to talk to me and try and make me feel at home. I think Micky Dove was honest in his assessment of me, but I really don't think anyone else at West Ham rated me.

From day one, I felt like I was on the outside looking in. It started early on. I had only been there a few months and the tickets to matches stopped coming, but it was the underhand way things were done that was the most upsetting. Darren and Kevin would be called over for a private chat and would be slipped tickets for the next home game, but as they were my friends they told me straight away. Then there would be matches that I wouldn't be invited to play in. Again, it was done in a clandestine way as if they thought they could keep it a secret from me. In training, I might as well have not been there for the amount of attention I was given. Conversely, Kevin and Darren were always getting little bits of advice and support.

I could tell by Christmas that they weren't going to have me back for the next season. I should have just left, but this was my first football rejection and my pride wouldn't let me. I kept thinking I could change their minds. Besides, it was embarrassing to go back to my life and admit that I had failed. At that age I had become defined by football. For years, I was Pottsy who plays for Villacourt. Now all the St George's players became defined by the professional club we were at. Elliot Taylor who plays for Arsenal, Danny Wareham, Steve Roast and Jason Peters who play for Southampton and I was now Pottsy who plays for West Ham. It was often the first thing people would say to you: 'Oh yes, I know you, you play for West Ham.' It made you feel important, like you were famous. Often, the kids who said it looked at you like you *were* famous.

I dreaded the idea of having to say I didn't play for West Ham any more. Even worse was having to say they had released me. The looks on people's faces when they realised that I was now no different to anyone else. The very idea filled me with horror. There were also all those people who had told me that I would never make it as a footballer, and that the odds were astronomical so I should lower my targets. I have never liked people who put limits on children's ambitions. I am a great believer, even now, that if you want something enough and work hard enough anything is possible. The idea that these people would be smugly saying I told you so prevented me from giving up. My whole life I had wanted to prove them wrong, so to now prove them right would be a bitter pill to swallow.

I used to travel up to training with Darren, whose dad John used to drive us. The journey used to be the best part of my night. John was so funny, and we would spend the whole journey laughing. I could tell it was awkward sometimes for Darren after training when we would get back in the car and he had been given tickets or a tracksuit and I had nothing, but he was brilliant. He never once rubbed my nose in it, and I think he genuinely felt sorry for me. Before long we would be cracking up again and for a few moments I would forget how horrible the whole situation was.

What I should have done was just take it as a learning experience and use it to help me improve. But I was 13 years old. It felt like everything I ever wanted was slipping through my fingers. Away from West Ham, things were still going okay, but I was starting to go into my shell a little at St George's. I was still scoring goals, but I was starting to doubt myself. I would miss the odd chance through overthinking what I was doing. Worse than that, I stopped joining in with the banter and started to pull away from my friends. In my head, I thought everyone knew that it was going badly for me at West Ham. I felt sure that word would have got back. I imagined them looking at me differently and thinking about me in a lesser way. It seems crazy now, but at the time I was ashamed.

Then, at the end of the season, just before West Ham made the announcement of who was going to stay and who wasn't, there was a friendly between their team and St George's. This often happened at the end of the season. Lots of the London professional teams would invite us in for friendlies while trying to poach a few of our players. I think Darren and Kevin played for West Ham in that match, but I'm not sure. What I do know is I played for St George's and we won by about five or six goals, with me scoring four of them. I felt great, thinking that I had proven something by my performance. Sure enough, two weeks later we were all sat down in training and I was told that I was being asked back again for the next year.

Shocking.

Once again, I should have told them to stick it, and left while I had the higher ground.

But I didn't.

The next year was worse.

At the time, there was a young player coming through at West Ham called Steve Potts. He went on to play a lot of games for their first team. In that second year, I got called Steve more times than I did my own name. On another occasion, I had hurt my ankle and was getting laser treatment on it at the training ground. The physio forgot about me, and it literally burned a hole in my foot. My mum was fuming. If it happened now, you would sue them. I never even got an apology.

By now I was desperate in my attempts to impress but I was trying too hard. I didn't know what they wanted from me. I knew they didn't rate me, but I didn't know why. I didn't know what I should be doing differently. I started to make bad decisions, second-guessing myself. I was now turning into the player that they thought I was.

I barely spoke to anyone.

It had now seeped into my football everywhere. At St George's, I was missing chances I would normally have finished without even a second thought. I began to think that people were seeing what West Ham had seen in me. I was paranoid and thought everyone was talking about me. Even before I made a mistake, I was already thinking about what people would think if I did get something wrong. As a footballer it is a terrible place to be. You start doing things based on what happened previously, so you shoot when you should have passed. The next time you get the ball you need to forget about what just happened and just react to the new situation. But you are in your own head, you have already decided that next time you get it you are going to pass. It is a different situation, however, and this time you should have shot. In the end your head is spinning as you make one bad decision after another. It's why good players need an arrogance about them. I once asked Teddy Sheringham about it. I'd watched him in training and when he missed he didn't seem to care even when other players had a go at him.

'If midfielders scream at you when you miss a shot, what do you do?'

He said, 'Shoot again and then tell them to f*** off! They'll soon moan if you don't score any goals and they don't get their win bonus.'

Great advice that I could have done with back then.

But at this point, I was trying to please everybody, trying to show them that I was still a good player. Even my school team. I had always been the main player and we had been successful considering we could hardly get out a side most weeks. One of my best friends was a kid called Ross Evans, who played rugby but not football. Phoning him up on a Saturday morning to see if he could make up the numbers became a regular thing. My friends at school had always been really supportive of me. All of a sudden, my mates were talking about players at the other schools and how good *they* were. To make matters worse, at St George's my friends were still hitting the same levels as always. A month or two into the season a league select team was picked. I wasn't selected. It was first time I hadn't got on a team I tried out for. Eight of the St George's side were on it. This now meant that they were going away to play and train with the select team. They were having stories and jokes to talk about that I was no part of, and talking about players I didn't know. I withdrew even more.

It is a strange thing to fully understand, but the best young players at your age have a sort of fame. When I had been playing well everyone knew me. Kids I never knew would come up to me and talk about football. I now wasn't one of those players. I would hear about Ollie Morah, Mark Flatts, Kevin Fowler, Garry Flitcroft, Trevor Sinclair, Lee Clark; these were the players who were going to be the next big thing. I felt a million miles away from them. Darren Hancock, who was considered among these players, used to try and help, bringing me into the conversations, but I just found it tough. As bad as I felt off the pitch it was worse on it. It got to the point that I didn't want to put myself in positions where I could make a mistake. I would see a run that I should make but would not make it in case the ball came to me and I missed the opportunity. When I got the ball, I just wanted to get it to another player and not give it away. I don't think people were ever mean about me, but there was a definite change towards me from the players and parents. I had gone from being part of the in crowd to someone who needed their sympathy. 'Keep your head up.' 'Don't give up.' 'You'll be okay in the end.' They were meaning to help, but all it did was cement the idea that I was failing, and I was less than what I was before.

For years at Villacourt and St George's, there had been players who fell away. First, they would start to stick out in matches. Maybe they would not be quite quick enough, or just not improve at the same rate as everyone else. Then they wouldn't always get in the team. Then they would leave and you would never really see them again. We all felt sorry for them as we knew they had the same dream as us. But that was football; you move on. We were united by our goal to be a professional player, and they were no longer on that journey. In reality this was nonsense, and children develop at different stages. These players just needed a little time and support. At the start of this particular season, we had an unexpected drop-out as Kevin Horlock left us to join our biggest rivals, St Thomas Moore. The goldfish bowl of Villacourt and then St George's had become too much. His form had dropped a little, he had not grown much and physically was behind some of the players. It was a sad day when he left, as he had been one of the players who had been there from the start. Now there were only four of us left.

Then there were the trials for Lilleshall School of Excellence.

It was a reasonably new thing where a squad of young players from all over the country went to the same school. They were then trained every day by England coaches. The idea was to ensure a bright future for English football. The ultimate aim was that it would produce a crop of players who would push England to the front of international football. It wasn't without its successes: Michael Owen, Sol Campbell, Nick Barmby, Jamie Carragher, Jermain Defoe, Andy Cole and Gareth Barry to name a few. It had a good rate of success; in academy football you would expect 0.5 per cent to actually make it as a professional. Out of 234 players who attended the school over the 15 years, 15 of them went on to represent England – that's 6.4 per cent. Ultimately, the lack of tournament success means the Lilleshall scheme was deemed a failure and closed in 1999.

Anyway, I didn't even get past the first trial. Yet another signpost showing everyone that I no longer belonged. What was worse was no one seemed surprised. Meanwhile, a lot of the St George's players went a long way in the process and three were all set to graduate. One, Danny Wareham, didn't make it due to discipline issues. He was a bit wild at that age and got in a bit of trouble when staying up at Lilleshall for one of the trials. No one really got the full facts, but knowing Danny there was probably a girl involved. Another one, Steve Roast, turned it down as he didn't want to leave his school. Steve was always very strong mentally and had his own opinions on things. I admired him for not following the crowd and always doing what he thought was best for him. He used to run the professional clubs a merry dance as they tried to sign him. For me, his approach is a great model for young players. Don't sign up with the clubs too early. Enjoy your football and let them chase you. In a period when we were all training at professional clubs, Steve improved more than anyone else just by playing football with his mates and doing his own thing. He actually went on to have a successful career playing in Sweden. The third was Darren Hancock. He did accept his place. He was now boarding in Shropshire which in turn meant my mum had to start making the long journey twice a week to take me to West Ham training, which I hated doing. It was ridiculous, but I was unable to admit defeat. Without Darren things were even worse. It felt like I was slowly disappearing altogether. By the end of the season, I was like a zombie walking through my own life, unable to change anything that was happening to me. I genuinely think I was suffering from depression, at 14. I began to get substituted by St George's for the first time, and then I never made the starting team. Finally, the inevitable came: a letter through the post telling me I was being released by West

Ham. My biggest surprise was that it was Anthony Potts not Steve Potts written on it. Two years of misery and they couldn't even tell me to my face.

I was now the only player at St George's without a professional club and I was about to enter the final two years of my education. I had never considered a life without football. I was a poor student. I mucked around and never put in any effort. I hadn't done any homework for two years; I used to copy everyone's homework before school and I spent most of my school life avoiding teachers who I owed work to. I was a good writer and mathematician, but never applied myself. Anyone who knew me at this age would be shocked to know I ended up being a teacher. Most of my teachers would probably hope that I had an Anthony Potts in my classes so that I got a taste of my own medicine.

It was a familiar problem. In primary school I was always one of the strongest students, but at a grammar school I was a small fish in a big pond. There were children there so much cleverer than me, and genuinely passionate about learning. If I couldn't be the best then I wasn't interested. I would rather fail not trying than put myself out there and still fail. My teachers must have hated me because I should have been doing so much better. My sister, Sarah, could have gone to Oxford and was an incredible student. She had a work ethic second to none that backed up her ability. I didn't. All of a sudden, I was now worrying about my grades. I had always presumed I wouldn't need them. I was so sure that my future was all mapped out for me. Now I was lost.

It was a crossroads in my life. I needed to do something, but I still had that thing that if I asked for help it meant I was admitting there was a problem. Like an alcoholic saying they need help. Eventually it got so bad that I had no choice, and I did what I should have done a long time before. I spoke to people. I spoke to my friends; I spoke to my family. It was like a weight being lifted and I should have done it two years previously. My friends were all very supportive, they actually believed in me more than I realised. My dad never watched me a great deal as a kid, and usually just came to cup finals. I actually think he thought children's football wasn't very good so why watch it? He watched me much more as an adult. He is one of the most honest people I know and would never sugar-coat something to me. He told me I wasn't strong enough, not confident enough, and that I was trying too hard to please everyone. My mum said I needed to step up at school and also thought I had given up and needed to fight for what I wanted. They were both right. We planned out what I was going to do. There was one more piece of advice from everyone.

I had to leave St George's.

6

Phoenix Rising

ONE OF the biggest changes I decided on was that I was no longer suited to being the main striker. My views on football had evolved. My favourite players were Glenn Hoddle, Charlie Nicholas, Kenny Dalglish and Peter Beardsley. I loved flair players. I wasn't overly quick and my strengths had changed: I was good with my back to the opponent's goal, I had a decent touch and I could spot a pass. I was really more of a number ten than a number nine. I started to watch videos of Kenny Dalglish and studied the areas he played in and the way he played. At times he was more like a midfielder than a forward. It meant I had to accept that I wasn't going to score as many goals!

My parents bought me a weights bench so that I could improve my strength, and my dad set me up a programme to work on. Every night I would do my circuit before going to bed. I would also do step-ups on the stairs and used to do hundreds of sit-ups and press-ups every day.

At school, much to the surprise of my teachers (and my friends) I started to pay attention and my grades began to improve. I even began to do my own homework. I still wasn't great, I would still get bored and muck about, but I did get the work done first. I can remember my maths teacher Mrs Gentry didn't trust my change of attitude. I had always been good at maths but never did the work, but I was now getting the work done and then doing my homework before the end of the lesson. My friend James Bray would sometimes now copy my work rather than the other way around, like it had been for years previously. When Mrs Gentry marked our books, she wrote 'great work' on James's book and wrote on mine, 'Stop copying James Bray.'

The next part of my plan needed me to find a club where I could work on my game without the pressure of results. In my school team were Simon Chapman and Gary Beerling, who played for Phoenix, a local side. They were both really nice kids, who I never heard say a bad word about anyone in all the time I knew them. They were just the kind of team-mates I needed. Phoenix played in a lower league than ours but were still a decent side. Gary's dad Mick was the manager and that's how I got involved.

The first few months of the season didn't go well. In my first game, I was booked for getting in a tussle with another player. It was the result of a rivalry from my Villacourt days and I thought nothing of it, but after the game I found out that it was the first booking that Phoenix had ever received. They had been together for about five years so it was an inauspicious start to my time with them. The first few months were quite tough. I was being selfish and didn't care whether we won or lost because I saw every match like a training session. I would work on different parts of my game. I started by working on my dribbling as by the end of my time at St George's I was too nervous to try and take people on, just choosing to do the easy thing, so I knew it was something I needed to improve on. In that first month at Phoenix, every time I got the ball I would try and take on my defender. I'm sure the other players weren't impressed. More often than not I would lose possession and it must have been frustrating for them. But developing a thicker skin was on my list of targets so I ignored their complaints and kept dribbling. Then every night I would be up the heath practicing my dribbling skills. I would also study the players on the television, looking at how they moved with the ball. Eventually I felt like I could always beat the first defender when I dribbled, so I went on to my next target: shooting.

I started to shoot. I would shoot from anywhere regardless of where my team-mates were. At first, the gardens behind the goal would be in more danger than the goal itself, but gradually I improved. I worked on getting my head over the ball, kicking right through it, bending the ball with the inside and outside of my foot and everything I could think of. Hours up on the heath, trying different techniques and making adjustments.

Up to this point, I was lucky to keep my place in the team. There were actually some very good players and I was getting by on reputation alone. It was quite insulting to use them like I did. One player in particular was clearly very talented: Sean Devine, who was quick and was a great finisher. But he looked disinterested and was lazy, and used to just stay out on the wing and not get involved. He is a great example to any young player as at the age of 16 he was still playing Sunday football yet he went on to carve out a great career in the professional game. I would cross paths with him later on in my career as our stars were heading in completely different directions.

In those early matches, I could see Gary's dad looking at me wondering if he had made a mistake. Luckily he stuck with me, based more on reputation than performance. Then things began to click. My shots started going in and we started winning games, and by Christmas I felt like I could do no wrong. I was starting to score some ridiculous goals. I may not have been scoring as many as I used to, but the quality of them was better and the quality of my all-round game was also much better. I had found myself actually enjoying assisting on goals as much as I did scoring them. It was like a revelation.

My weights programme was starting to take effect too. My calves in particular had seemed to grow beyond belief, and were Kenny Sansom-esque! What it meant was I could hold off defenders and shield the ball under pressure. I had also gained a little bit of explosive pace from them so had become quicker over the first few yards; I was like a different player. As the season went on, we started to look like a good side. We had a very good keeper called Greg Smith and with Sean's goals and my new-found form we climbed the league.

I loved my time there and made lots of friends. I can remember playing with a lad called Alex Simms. I had played against him loads of times and every team I played for hated him as he was a bit of a dirty player and never shut up. He always knew what to say to really push people's buttons. Playing in the same side as him was great fun, though. You soon realised that he just loved winding people up. He really didn't care and he had to have eyes in the back of his head to avoid all the players who spent most of the game trying to kick him.

In the end, there was one very strong team in our league and we just couldn't beat them, finishing runners-up to them in the table and getting knocked out of both cup competitions by them. If I'm honest, I didn't care. My focus was completely on my career. I knew I was playing well, better than I ever had, but no scouts were coming to watch us play. At St George's there would be scouts there every week but at Phoenix we were lucky if we got one man and his dog. At the end of the season, I had no choice and it was back to St George's I went.

7

Is F*** an Adverb?

THE ST George's team I returned to was much changed from the one I had left. The players who had been offered schoolboy forms at their professional clubs were no longer allowed to play Sunday football, which meant that they had a completely different side. The new manager's name was Mick and he also ran a building company. He was a no-nonsense kind of a bloke. I used to find his team talks hilarious as I had never heard someone use the word f*** so much in my life. He would use it as a verb, noun, adjective and adverb all in one sentence. 'F***ing pass the f***ing f***er or I will f*** my f***ing f***.'

I honestly didn't have a clue what he was saying. I would just sit there and nod. The team was supposed to be under-16s but he had brought in three ringers from his building firm, who all played under aliases. We had a very physical and strong team and overpowered most of our opponents that year. On the wing we had a player called Austin Berkley, who was frustrating to play with but was one of the best dribblers I had ever seen. As a forward you would make a run and he would see you, but he'd just carry on dribbling the ball. I now knew what the Phoenix players must have felt like the year before. But there was no denying his ability. He ended up becoming a professional and among other clubs he played nearly 200 games for Shrewsbury Town. I had a friend who played in the same side as him during a spell at Swindon Town and they told me that the whole team used to try and kick him in training as they couldn't get the ball off him! Apparently, it resembled a scene out of *Benny Hill* with a line of players chasing him around the field. We also had a kid in midfield called Bradley, I think, who ended up getting signed by Gillingham at the end of the year. He was a very good passer and set up a lot of goals for me that year. I played up front and was pretty much left alone to do my own thing.

In the pre-season we entered a tournament, although the rest of the teams involved were adults. Bearing in mind I hadn't exactly covered myself in glory my last season at the club, expectations were low. But to say I hit the floor running was an understatement, as we won the competition and I scored in every game. I surprised myself with how well I played. For one of the goals, I was clean through on the goalkeeper and I did a step over that sent him diving in completely the wrong direction. I then rolled the ball into the empty goal. It was audacious and, that moment, the confidence it gave me set me up for the season. We won everything that year and my form continued.

Moving back to St George's proved to be a wise choice as I soon had scouts ringing me up most weeks offering me a trial. I actually kept a football diary that year because I had a feeling it was going to be a special season. I played 96 games and scored 162 goals. Looking back, the amount of games I played was ridiculous. I would have played more than 100 but I missed a few with an injured knee. It was far too many to play but I could do no wrong and I was addicted to the way I felt every time I stepped on the pitch, and I had also been playing at least as many games from the age of eight through to 15 at Villacourt so I was used to it. In truth it wasn't healthy and probably contributed to my later problems, but I was loving life and couldn't get enough. It felt like I was proving everyone wrong, throwing their doubts back down their throats. I would play for anyone who asked.

Millwall, Chelsea, Arsenal, Crystal Palace, Charlton, Southampton, Liverpool and Tottenham all contacted me in the first few months of that season, desperate to get me to sign for them, and I loved the attention I was getting. The more people praised me the better I played. In the footballing circles that I played in, it was like I just landed from Mars. Here I was, 15 years old, in my last year at school and I was the best player every week no matter who I played for.

The reception I was getting was a mixture of surprise and admiration. To observers it was literally an overnight thing but for me it was the culmination of a year's hard work. An example would be the trials for the Kent under-19 side just after the start of the season. My school sent me along, but most people had already written me off as I had been off the 'scene' for so long. When I turned up, I could tell that I was like lift muzak as people were pleased that I was there but the expectations were low. The day was a series of matches, with the under-19 managers watching along with scouts from half the professional teams in London. I was the best player there. These are my memoirs so I can say what I think, and I hope I have been honest, my aim has been to be brutally honest. I am not being big-headed. I was head and shoulders above everyone there that day.

I can remember Danny Wareham coming up to me at the end of the first game. We hadn't seen each other since I left St George's. He had a look of shock on his face and he told me that it must have been the best I had ever played. He meant it as a compliment; Danny has always been a good friend, but it made me laugh as I had been playing at that level for nearly six months by this point. In the final trial, I scored a goal where I dribbled past four or five players. My old team-mates from Villacourt were looking at me like I was an imposter; I never used to do things like that. I was normally the player just getting on the end of things.

When the day had finished, I was inundated with phone calls from scouts wanting me to go training with their clubs. I said yes to everyone. My intention had always been to play the field and enjoy the attention. It was on this day that I first caught the eye of the Spurs scout, Tony Hacket. Tony had known me for years as his son Ben used to train with Villacourt back when he was still in primary school. Tony's whole family were football-mad and would always be there at every event. Tony had a stunned look on his face. He told me he never knew I had that in me, and explained he was now scouting for Tottenham, and that Ben was playing for the under-15s there. He thought that they would love me at Spurs as I was just the sort of player they had been signing in recent years. He really sold the club to me. I said I would go training, but we parted not having arranged anything concrete. To be honest, I think Tony may have thought it was a fluke. I can't stress enough the difference in me from just a year and a bit before. No one had seen the bit in between; it must have confused everyone. If it was in professional sports then they would have been testing me for drugs.

My season just kept going from strength to strength and in November I played for the Junior Reds, which is a team affiliated to Charlton Athletic. I don't even know how it happened, but I was enjoying my football so much at this stage that I would play for anyone who asked. We played at Sincil Bank, Lincoln City's home ground. Lincoln were playing Charlton in a friendly afterwards and our game was like a warm-up for the main event. I loved it; the pitch was immaculate and the longer the game went on the more people turned up to watch it. Everything I tried that day worked. I can remember going on one run that took me the whole length of the pitch and it was only a good save that stopped me scoring at the end of it, although we won 6-0 and I did score a couple.

Charlton were watching the game, and they got in touch and asked me to come down to training. Initially there was some confusion about the date they wanted me and I took it as meaning they weren't that keen – probably still an insecure remnant from my West Ham days. As a result, I wrote them off and didn't turn up for training. In the meantime, Tottenham came back in for me. Tony Hacket had turned up and watched me play for St George's, which must have confirmed to him that my trial performance hadn't been a one-off. At that stage I was being chased by several teams as an unattached 16-year-old playing at the level I was is very unusual. Tottenham were very keen and invited me down for a game with their under-16 side. It was so professional. We played in the proper kit and it was all laid out under our pegs. We had a physio, manager and a coach. It was my first glimpse of football at a different level. When the other team turned up, it was Charlton!

I had a very good game and scored a goal with a nice finish. The style of football was perfect for me. It was based on quick clever passing, and I felt at home immediately. My dad came along to watch and was very impressed when he heard the Tottenham coaching staff talking about one of their players,

Kevin Watson. They were really pleased that in the game he had started to do something that they had wanted to see from him for a while. My dad didn't know what the thing was, but he loved the fact that they were actually trying to develop their players. Kevin went on to have a great career, the foundations for which were built at Tottenham.

At the end of the game, they invited me to go training with them, and I said I would love to. That night I got a phone call from Charlton, but I told them that I thought they hadn't seemed keen. They explained that the reason they were uncertain over training was that Alan Curbishley, the first team manager, wanted to be there to meet me. He had watched the Junior Reds game and been impressed with what he saw, so he had hoped that by stepping in himself he could convince me to sign for Charlton. He had not been happy when he turned up and I wasn't there. They still wanted to sign me, and in fact after my performance against them they were even more keen. Unfortunately, by now I had my head turned by Spurs, and went for my first training session with them on the Tuesday. We trained at White Hart Lane in a ball court just outside the stadium and we changed in the actual changing rooms. I loved it. There were some very talented players, and it was clear that they wanted me there. I had more praise in two hours than I had had in two years at West Ham.

Incredibly, in a strange moment of coincidence, my second appearance for the under-16 side was against West Ham at Mill

Hill, the Tottenham training ground. I could not have been any more motivated.

Before the game, the manager had told the team to play through me as much as possible and said some really complimentary things. It made me feel wanted and I felt on top of the world when I took to the pitch; we won 3-1 and I scored again. More importantly I ran them ragged. Some players respond well to criticism and some to praise. I have always been the latter. If I feel that I have a team's trust, the pressure to impress lifts and I just play my game. The opinion of my team-mates has always meant a lot to me.

Once again, my dad had positioned himself near the managers. Halfway through the second half I went on a good run, beating a couple of players and setting up a chance. The manager on the sideline turned to Jimmy Frith, who was their coach, and commented that the number ten was a good player and asking whether he knew if I had been signed by Spurs yet. Jimmy had to explain that West Ham had released me a year and a half before. Finally, a bit of closure.

I also had another introduction to the complicated world of football in that game. Unbeknown to me, Spurs had a series of code words that meant different things. If someone said 'Sid', you back-heeled the ball, and if they said 'Jack' you dummied it. There were a couple of others but they escape me now. They were all boys' names. Anyway, in the first half the ball was passed to me on the edge of the box and one of the players shouted 'Jack'. My name's Tony so I ignored it and took the shot, only to be treated to a mouthful by the player who had been calling for me to dummy the ball. For a good five minutes he was moaning at me, thinking I had been greedy by ignoring him. It was only at half-time, when I was able to explain that I didn't know the code, that he forgave me.

After the game, I went to watch the first team play. It had been just over a year since the famous 1986/87 Tottenham side with Ray Clemence, Chris Hughton, Garry Mabbutt, Clive Allen, Paul Allen, Glenn Hoddle, Ossie Ardiles, Steve Hodge, Chris Waddle, Nico Claesen and Richard Gough had finished third in the First Division and were runners-up in the FA Cup. Tottenham fans would still be able to name the majority of that squad, even now. It was the year Clive Allen scored 49 goals and Tottenham played some unbelievable football.

But the season immediately after that, which was the one just before I joined, had not been such a good one for Spurs. The iconic Hoddle left for Marseille, Ardiles went to Blackburn Rovers, Allen was sold to Bordeaux, Gough joined Rangers, Hodge moved to Nottingham Forest and Claesen signed for Antwerp. David Pleat was also sacked after being cited three times for kerb-crawling. Terry Venables had taken over at the end of November and Spurs finished a disappointing 13th, so a serious rebuilding programme was needed. The three Pauls – Gascoigne, Walsh and Stewart – were brought in, but the new campaign had started poorly. By the end of October, Spurs were in the bottom three and Venables was under pressure, but by December the team had recovered well, Gazza was starting to find his feet and Chris Waddle's recent form had been outstanding.

It was the first time that I saw Gazza play. It was amazing. Waddle was also in the side, and it was like a game of one-upmanship. It was football on a different level. The two of them were head and shoulders above anything I had ever seen live. Gascoigne was mesmerising. He could do everything. He had a great range of passing, one minute playing clever little one-twos and the next releasing a 40-yard ball with pinpoint accuracy. He also went past people as if they weren't there, with his incredible change of pace and fast feet. He was also very powerful; no one could knock him off the ball. He even won a few tackles and headers. It was the best individual performance I had ever seen, and Waddle wasn't far behind.

Gazza also did the full comedy routine with sticking tape to the referee's back, hiding the ball up his top, kicking the ball at the mascot and generally looking like he was having the time of his life. I went home that night buzzing from my day. My face ached from smiling, and I finally felt like my dream was back on course.

Spurs fit me like a glove. From the minute I got there I felt at home. I had been an Arsenal supporter since the age of five, but the fact is that as my knowledge of football grew, I liked their style of football less and less. I could trace it all the way back to the 1982 World Cup. That was the year that Brazil should have won it. They played football of the kind I had never seen. Every player was comfortable on the ball and there was a swagger about their play. Zico, Sócrates, Júnior, Éder; the names will live with me forever. The goals they scored were breathtaking, but in the end it was defensive errors and the great finishing of Italy's Paulo Rossi that was to deny them. Supporting Arsenal, I certainly wasn't seeing anything like it. That Brazil team inspired a generation of footballers and I don't think I ever looked at the game quite the same way after that World Cup.

Arsenal had hit a serious slump after the three consecutive FA Cup finals that had started me off supporting them. Then George Graham joined them from Millwall in 1986, and over the next couple of seasons he had done a tremendous rebuilding job. The problem was it was based heavily on defence; '1-0 to the Arsenal' had become a familiar chant. During the barren years, my one saving grace had been Charlie Nicholas. He had scored a bundle of goals in Scotland for Celtic and everyone expected him to join Manchester United or Liverpool, but it was a real shock when he signed for Arsenal and a new hero had arrived for me. I even got a haircut like his. In truth, he was lazy and I used to cringe when I saw him not even bother to jump and try and win a header. But he had quality. He played a similar style to Kenny Dalglish, and the crowd loved him. I actually saved my money and bought a season ticket for Arsenal the year I was at Phoenix, based mainly on wanting to see him play live. I was devastated when they sold him after just three games of that season. Myself, Richard Boyce and Marcello Giovanelli (two friends from school) used to go to every home game. We also travelled to Liverpool to watch us lose 2-0. Secretly, I was more looking forward to seeing the Liverpool team play live than I was watching Arsenal. It was a great team that played exhilarating football, and it was a day memorable for an exquisite Peter Beardsley goal that I applauded while standing among the hardcore Arsenal away support. Richard grabbed my arms to stop me clapping, scared that we were going to get beaten up. I was enjoying Arsenal's success but I hated the football.

Tottenham, though, was different. I loved their style of play and it suited me perfectly, and they clearly felt I suited them too. At training I used to wear my Arsenal kit at first, but it soon seemed a bit of a churlish gesture. I was also now experiencing life on the other side of the fence. At training I would be the one getting pulled aside for little discussions. I was the one getting tickets and tracksuits. I felt uncomfortable. It seemed so cut-throat. A lot of that Tottenham under-16 side had been together for years, coming through the system. There were already strong friendship groups. Being the top youth team in the country, Tottenham were able to attract the most talented players from London and beyond. These players had been originally chased by Spurs and you could see that for some of them it was all slipping through their fingers. I could see in some of them what had happened me at West Ham. They knew that the club had lost interest in them.

They say there is no loyalty in football and they are right. At 15 and 16 they were still kids and deserved better. The system was rigged against the player. If you signed schoolboy forms then the club could still release you, but you couldn't leave. Also, if they offered you YTS forms at the end of the schoolboy forms then you had to sign them. Personally, I was riding on a crest of a wave but it wasn't pleasant seeing some of these loyal players being released. Don't get me wrong, everyone was very friendly towards me, even those players who were being released. They welcomed me like a club would a new signing. It was football, you move on. Footballers can be fickle; the better players saw that I could play and that was good enough for them. They could also see that the club rated me, so I was accepted immediately. It was still hard seeing players experiencing what I had experienced at West Ham.

Over the Christmas holidays, I was invited in to train with the youth team at the training ground. It was a sign of how well things had been going as not many players got invited. This was the first time I had seen some of the other under-16 players. Being one of the top youth teams in the country meant that Spurs had signed players from all over the country. There were strong links with Ireland as Spurs had been recruiting heavily there, and there were four or five Irish players at training that week. There were also the Lilleshall boys who were home for Christmas. Tottenham were heavily represented at Lilleshall with at least five players in every year group. Involved that year there were Sol Campbell, Nick Barmby, Darren Caskey and Ollie Morah among others, and they were all in at training over Christmas. Jamie Redknapp was also there as he lived in Bournemouth, so didn't train during term time. I was petrified! All the first team players would be there, as well as the reserve and the youth teams. My whole time at Spurs was very much like that. You would be scared and excited at exactly the same time. Being around famous footballers was a buzz, but you were desperate not to show yourself up. Greg Howell was an under-16 player like me. His dad was Ron Howell, who used to play for Millwall, and my dad had recognised him at the West Ham game. Greg knew everyone, and I spent the two weeks listening intently to everything he said.

In the youth team the top player was a lad called Shaun Murray, who apparently was the most highly rated young player in the country. He was from Newcastle, and I watched him closely in training. He looked a good player but it gave me hope that if he was the best and two years older than me, then maybe I did have a chance. The youth team players from different parts of the country lived in digs. This was basically like a bed and breakfast. You had your room and the person who owned the digs did all your meals and washing for you. I read later that Shaun had struggled with being away from home. I almost feel guilty now with how I judged players at that time. According to Greg, another youth team player to watch out of the second-years was Peter Garland. Peter was another larger-than-life character. He always had a story and was right in the middle of everything. In the end I think it was only injuries that stopped him going to the very top.

The under-16s trained with the first-year YTS team. Out of the first-year YTS boys, I already knew Kevin and Neil Smith as they played the year above me at county football for Kent. Kevin in particular had a huge reputation and in training you could see he had a lot of ability. They also had several players who had been at Lilleshall and who played for the England youth team. Among them were Scott Houghton, Ian Walker and Ian Hendon, who had been the England captain at schoolboy level. In youth team training that week were four players – Walker, Redknapp, Barmby and Campbell – who were all to go on to play for England. I guess it puts the Lilleshall statistics into a little more context.

I spent the two weeks trying to learn as much as I possibly could. The best bit was getting a glimpse of the life of a professional footballer. It was a wonderful two weeks. You only really got glimpses of the first team players training as we were training at the same time across the field from them. They also would finish before us most days, although a few would stay after training, including Paul Gascoigne. The first team players were loud and confident. They seemed to really enjoy training and they were always joking around. It made we want to be a professional even more. They were getting paid to play football and have a laugh with their mates every day, and most days they were finished by 12.

One of my biggest shocks was how good some of the lesser-known players were. Vinny Samways and John Moncur in particular were so talented. In some ways they were unlucky to be at the club at the same time as Paul because they were similar kind of players. Vinny, in training and in reserve games, was nothing like the Vinny who would appear for the first team. He could run quicker with the ball than without it, was incredibly gifted and a good finisher. He should have done so much more than he did with his career, and he stayed at Spurs longer than he should have. The fans used to call him 'Vinny Sideways' as he always took the easy option, which was a shame as he had so much more to offer. John was the son of John Moncur senior, the youth development officer, and was another player who stayed too long. That Christmas, there was talk that Brian Clough wanted to buy him for Nottingham Forest and that could have been the making of him. In the end, John stayed at Spurs for eight years, but he only played 24 games in those eight years. In fairness, he still ended up having a great career with Swindon and West Ham despite those lost years.

I held my own at training in those two weeks and I could tell I had been accepted by the other players. It was easy to tell; if they passed the ball to you, then they thought you were a decent player. There were some who were clearly out their depth and you could tell the others didn't trust them. They barely got passed to. Those two weeks were a great confidence boost. I had played and trained with some of the best young players in the country and had not looked out of place. It felt like I was as good as anyone there, and the coaches seemed to think so too.

After training over Christmas, I was put into the club's South East Counties Division Two side. At this point, I should explain how the youth system was set up at Spurs. Each year they tried to take on a whole team of new YTS players, who were paid £29.50 a week and given a two-year contract. In the first year they were expected to make up the B team in the South East Counties Division Two. In their second year, they would want to be in the A squad, playing in the South East Counties Division One. You knew you were doing well if you could play above your expected level, and if you did that then you would generally be expected to get a professional contract, but only a handful of players were signed at the end of the two years. Professional contracts were like gold dust. I will talk about it from the professional's viewpoint later in the book.

Tottenham at the time had the best youth set-up in the country. They had won the South East Counties League for five years on the spin and had invested heavily in youth. For me as a schoolboy, I should have been playing in the under-16 side, but had leapfrogged straight into the B team. In my first game there were only two players who were not YTS trainees:

myself and a certain Jamie Redknapp. We struck up a great friendship that year as the only two schoolboys to regularly play in that side. Jamie had even played a few games in the A team earlier in the season. He was without a doubt the best player I had played with up to that point. With his background he was completely relaxed and at home at a professional club. He had been skipping school and joining in training with the first team at a Harry Redknapp-managed Bournemouth since the age of 13. His technique was unreal. In training over Christmas, his passing and shooting was crisper and sharper than everyone else, including a lot of the first team. I used to try and copy him, study how he struck the ball. I became a better player just from playing and training with him.

The B team manager was Pat Holland and he was tough, especially with the YTS boys. He had been a winger for West Ham and was always talking about Trevor Brooking. Pat was a brilliant coach and I learned so much from him. He was always taking me aside for extra training and talking about my game and what I needed to do to improve. It was a big learning curve for me as I had never really been coached before. The YTS players were training every day and were far more knowledgeable than me. I had to pick it up fast or I would have stuck out like a sore thumb. It was awkward too, because by playing a level up me and Jamie were taking the place of a YTS trainee, one of the friends of the other YTS players. You can imagine being at work and having a great friend then someone turns up to take their place. It would be easy to be resentful. It put more pressure on me to play well because if you didn't then it would make them feel like you shouldn't be there. There were players who were not happy to see me and Jamie in the team. I used to travel to matches with Neil Carey, who was a first-year YTS boy. He and his dad were brilliant with me, and I really appreciated their help. Neil was not enjoying the best of starts to his YTS and it was a tough time for him. Meanwhile I was going from strength to strength. Lesser people could have resented me, but Neil isn't that kind of a person and he actually helped me with my game. He left at the end of that season to complete his YTS at Norwich.

Before playing in the youth team, I had thought I knew a lot about football. In reality I knew nothing. I can honestly say from the first second at Spurs, my real education began. I was like a sponge and I tried to soak it all up. They explained my role in the team and told me exactly what was expected from me. In the past, I had just gone out and played. I ran where I thought the space was or where I thought the ball would be. All of a sudden, I realised that I had to be in certain places at certain times. If I wasn't there then the players would moan at me as they all knew where I should be too. I had to learn quickly, but I enjoyed the process. It was the same when defending, and I had specific jobs to do. Normally I would just run about and try and get the ball back when we had lost it. Now I had to do my job as part of the whole team, which was hard to grasp at first, but when you did it correctly you got a real sense of achievement.

My first game against Charlton had been in the middle of December, and at the start of January I was asked to stay behind after training. This wasn't unusual as I had clearly become one of their favourites. I would often get gifts or tickets or just words of encouragement. John Moncur senior was there and he gave me a long talk about how impressed they had been and then told me that they wanted to sign me on schoolboy forms for the rest of the season. At West Ham, I had longed to be signed on schoolboy forms but never came close. This was different though, because I had been playing out of my skin, and I knew how highly Spurs thought of me. I said no as I wanted to keep my options open. Immediately he offered me YTS forms for the following two seasons. I nearly bit his hand off and signed there and then in the changing rooms. I thought I had been clever not signing as a schoolboy but the fact he had the YTS forms waiting there suggested that I wasn't as clever as I thought. When I later spoke to the other players, they were shocked that all I got was a YTS deal. It turned out that most of the players who had signed YTS forms got money, or a car, or a guarantee of a professional contract. They knew how well liked I was and had presumed I got the same! But I didn't care, I wasn't interested in money, I would have played for nothing. I was back on track and I now knew that I had two and a half years to prove to Tottenham that I was worthy of a professional contract.

By the time the next holiday came about, I was playing every week for the B team and had scored a few goals too. Jamie and I had built up a good understanding and it was going well, but the holidays were to prove a strange time. The good bit was I was invited back into the training ground to train with the youth team again. The bad news was that the players returning from Lilleshall and Ireland needed matches so I was relegated to the substitutes' bench for the B team. I fully understood because Pat Holland took the time to explain the situation to me. They needed to see how these players were developing and they only had a limited amount of games they could play in. I didn't mind too much and I was interested to see how good they were.

Ollie Morah took my place in the starting side. I already knew of him through the grapevine when I was at Villacourt. He had a reputation for scoring goals and was one of the players being regularly talked about. He was over six feet tall and was ripped despite never having lifted a weight in his life. By all accounts, he had been about the same size since the age of ten. He was also lightning quick. Because he played up front, I saw him as my competition, and in a way he was, although in truth we were very different players. I was pleased that when I came on, I managed to score a goal as I wanted him to think of me as an equal and to show everyone that he was no better than me. My old Kevin Horlock competitiveness was already coming out.

This holiday was also an interesting one for giving me an insight into Sol Campbell. Sol was two years younger and had already been earmarked for great things. He and Danny Hill from their age group were the top two players. Danny was an incredibly talented player for his age who would sometimes play two years above himself in the B team, and would look like one of the best players even then. I always thought that he would go on to great things when he made his debut for Spurs at 18 and looked equally at home. He actually played in the derby against Arsenal when he was still only 19 and ran the show. It can be peculiar how some players just drift away.

I remember that holiday that there was a game arranged, and with all the Lilleshall boys and the Irish boys being available competition for places was tight. There were about 40 of us standing around at the end of training as the squad was announced. When I heard my name read out, I had to stifle a cheer as I was so pleased. When they read out Sol's name, he didn't seem too bothered. Pat Holland noticed this and said that he didn't have to play if he didn't want to. Pat was being sarcastic, trying to get across to Sol that he should have been pleased as he was basically playing two years above himself and that there were about 20 players standing there who would have loved to have been selected. Sol just said he wouldn't play then as he wanted to chill out over the holidays! But this was Sol to a tee. He was the most laid-back person you were ever likely to meet. At the time, he was playing in central midfield, but he was a good centre-forward and could also play at the back. It all came easy to him and the club loved him. I know he is hated by Tottenham fans for his defection to Arsenal. The truth is he would not have even considered the consequences. He probably just felt, quite rightly at the time, that he had more chances of getting silverware at Arsenal so he went. He wasn't the type to overthink things and was probably shocked when he got as much stick as he did. I would also imagine that as long as he didn't change too much from when I knew him, it probably didn't bother him too much either. Everyone liked Sol for his chilled-out persona and you would never hear a bad word said about him.

When the Lilleshall players went back, things returned to normal and I finished the season as a regular starter for the B team. I played up front with a lad called Hung Dang. He was a Vietnamese refugee with incredible technique and the biggest legs I had ever seen. He was a real rags to riches story. I once saw an interview with Andy Cole where he spoke about Hung Dang as an example of a player who looked like he had everything but did nothing. There is actually more to the story. That season, Hung Dang injured his knee and, when they did a scan, they found out he had no cruciate ligament – a birth defect. It was a mystery that he could even walk let alone play football. They thought it was only his huge leg muscles that had kept his legs together that long. I believe he was forced to retire.

At the end of the season, the under-16s went on tour to France to play in a huge tournament. Ajax and Barcelona were also taking part and there were a lot of players who went on to great things. We came up against some fantastic teams. The level of expectation was raised even higher during the trip, and you could tell they were preparing you for the harsher world of full-time training. It was the last chance for some players to earn their YTS contracts and there was a lot of pressure on the matches. We did quite well and ended up getting through to the semi-final but eventually lost on penalties. Jamie and I both missed our penalties in the shoot-out and at the end of the game Pat Holland really laid into the two of us. It was the first rollocking I had ever had in football, and it was tough. I can remember sitting there staring at the floor trying not to cry as Pat shouted abuse in my face. At one point he screamed at me to look at him while he shouted at me. It was a real effort just to keep back the tears and I know Jamie felt the same.

After the match, John Moncur senior took us to one side as he could see we were upset. He explained that it was part of football, and that we should learn from it and not take it too much to heart. It was excellent advice and a good lesson learned. I think John, as development officer, knew we were good players and didn't want us to get the hump and walk away. Nowadays you can't treat young players like that as they will just switch off or leave. Back then it was the norm. Young players were often treated appallingly, and everyone had been in a changing room where someone had been physically threatened by their manager or coach. In my opinion there are two sides to it. I don't doubt that some coaches and managers crossed the line, but I think in the long run it led to mentally stronger players. If you could survive the abuse, then mentally you could deal with anything. But that doesn't make it right, though, in the wider picture.

It was on this trip that it became clear that Jamie wanted to leave Spurs and stay with his dad at Bournemouth. He spoke to me about joining him at Bournemouth, as Harry liked me as a player, but I was loving my life at Spurs so it was never an option. He also tapped up Greg Howell, who was an excellent player in the mould of Glenn Hoddle, and it looked like Greg would join him. Greg, though, was an Enfield boy, lived minutes away from White Hart Lane and was too comfortable at home so didn't join Jamie in the end. Terry Venables was fuming when he heard that Jamie wanted to leave. Apparently, he and Harry had a huge row as Venables clearly knew what a prospect Jamie was. In the end, Harry said that Jamie was homesick and that it wasn't a football decision so Venables agreed to tear up Jamie's contract. I am sure he must have hit the roof when less than two years later, Kenny Dalglish signed Jamie for Liverpool, 200 miles away from his home at Bournemouth!

There was another moment that left a bad taste in my throat on that trip. There was a young player at Spurs who at 14 had been one of the best prospects in the country. His name was Mark and the club had given him a huge contract that included a long professional deal after his YTS finished. The rumours were that his dad had been given a job at the club and that he had been given a large lump sum too. Unfortunately, Mark had stood still and not developed like expected. The club no longer believed in him. He was a shy, quiet kid and, on the trip, in a calculated move he did not play a second of football. When we returned, they called his dad into the office and told him that what had happened on the trip would be what would happen if he took up his contract. In the end he left.

The first team finished the season on good form. Chris Waddle was named in the team of the year and Paul Gascoigne made his debut for England, while sixth place was a respectable finish following their poor start. Hopes were high and with the announcement of Gary Lineker signing from Barcelona there was real optimism at the club. The Spurs fans needed cheering up as their bitter rivals from across north London won their first league title for nearly 20 years with practically the last kick of the season at Anfield against Liverpool. Despite my reservations on their style of football, I was overjoyed with my boyhood club finally winning a championship in my lifetime. As much as I admired the football of that Liverpool side, they only had themselves to blame. In the last few minutes you could see them high-fiving each other, and John Barnes must still regret his decision not to head for the corner flag in the final seconds. I can remember the mood at training that week was not good after Arsenal won the league, and I had to pretend to be as annoyed as everyone else.

8

Up for the Cup

THE OPTIMISM from the end of the last season was soon tested with the news that Chris Waddle was to be joining Glenn Hoddle in French football. I was hugely disappointed with the news that Chris was leaving Spurs for Marseille as I had been looking forward to seeing him in training. In my opinion, he had been the best player in England for the previous two seasons and he was sure to be a loss. I did manage to get his boots from the boot room when I knew he was leaving, which helped me get over it. I ended up selling them, but I wish that I had kept them now.

The good news was that Gary Lineker was joining from Barcelona along with an almost unnoticed Nayim. In a shrewd move, Terry Venables had insisted on Nayim being added into the deal that took Gary to the Camp Nou. In a hugely talented Spurs squad that year, he was technically by far the best. When I think back to his technical ability, it's what I would imagine a Messi or Maradona must have, but he just didn't have their pace or physicality. In training the youth team players would watch him in awe and there was nothing he couldn't do with a football. He actually became a legend with Spurs fans more for his goal from the halfway line against Arsenal to beat them in the European Cup Winners' Cup Final than he did for his obvious talent on the pitch.

Nayim had been at Barcelona when Diego Maradona had signed and saw him in training every day. Nayim swore that Maradona's technique was much better than his but I honestly couldn't see how. I once got a back-handed compliment in comparison to Nayim. Keith Waldon, who managed the South East Counties Division One side, spoke about how I was the best technical player in the youth team and yet my technique was far below that of Nayim's. Keith was using his comments as a way to get us to still work hard to improve our techniques. I still took it as a compliment because I hadn't seen anyone to compare with Nayim. You got the impression that Gazza may have been able to compete technically, but he was less smooth and more physical.

An interesting fact that shows you how the Spurs team was evolving was that just two years after the 1987 FA Cup Final, only four of the 14 players who took part were still at the club at the start of the 1989/90 season. That is one hell of a turnaround and shows the good job that Venables was doing.

That year, if I had a pound for how many times I was asked what Gazza and Gary Lineker were like, I would be a rich man right now. I will come to Gazza more later but this is a good time to tell you my thoughts on Gary. He took the art of goalscoring to a whole new level. He was like a machine that had been programmed to do one job: score goals. Everything he did from match to match was focused on that one target. In training during the week, he was only interested in parts of the session that helped him score more goals. While the other players would love to play five-a-side at the end of a session he would walk off to the changing rooms as he saw no benefit.

On long-distance runs he would put in no effort and practically jog around. We used to do a run around a park during pre-season, and in the middle of the park was a wooded area we ran through. We had to do two laps on what was a long run. He would hide in the trees on the first lap then join in on the second one. Finishing practices or speed work? Then he was completely focused as they would help him. He was a phenomenal finisher. As the season progressed you would notice a pattern; he would be injured early in the week for the harder sessions and would jog around the training ground and get massages in the physio room. Then, when the training got easier later in the week, he would join in on the parts he thought relevant to him. Venables managed him perfectly. He understood that, especially at that stage of his career, Lineker knew his art better than anyone so he gave him his head. He basically just left him to get on with it because week in and week out he did the business on the pitch.

In matches, every movement Gary made on the pitch was designed to give him an opportunity to score a goal. His movement off the ball was second to none. At the end of his first season with Spurs I bought the club video of his goals from the season as it was an education. He only made about four different runs, but they were all perfection. He would come short and signal with his hand in a circular motion, and then he would spin and sprint in behind. He got about five goals that year doing this. When the ball went out wide, he had two different runs. He would either start towards the near post then dart to the far, or start towards the far post then dart to the near. He scored about ten goals with those runs. His last run would be to pull on to the centre-half's shoulder for the ball over the top, and he scored four or five goals like that too. Add penalties and you had a guaranteed 20 goals a season striker.

You couldn't stop Gary, as his runs were timed to perfection and he was too quick for any defender to live with. When he got the ball in any of those positions there was only ever one outcome. He had ice in his veins. His conversion rate must have been incredible as he rarely missed. Again, though, if something didn't help him score a goal, he wasn't interested. At Tottenham at the time, defending the full-backs was the forward's job. Frankly it was a nightmare. If the ball got thrown out to the full-back you had to chase him all the way down the pitch and if you didn't you knew a rollocking was coming your way from everyone. But Lineker was on to that. He didn't want to waste precious energy that could be used on scoring goals. Any cross that was going to be intercepted by the keeper, he would come sliding in. To the crowd it would look like a player's desperate efforts to reach the ball, but we all knew better! It just meant that he never had to chase the full-back when the keeper threw out the ball. He would instead slowly get up off the floor looking forlorn at nearly scoring a goal. It was great acting.

He was also extremely clever when it came to the press. He was always very aware when the press were at the training ground and would stop and sign for every autograph hunter if a camera was nearby. That wasn't always the case on other days. He was clearly always destined for a career in media when he did finally retire. I don't mean to sound negative, as he was truly a player that I admired and I feel privileged to have seen him at work. Any aspiring forward should study his goals on YouTube. He was a player who was a master of his craft and completely dedicated to being the very best at what he did. He scored an incredible 221 goals in 406 games in English football. At Spurs he scored 80 in 138, all the more amazing when you consider he was 32 when he joined.

Life as a YTS player in the 1980s was very different to how it is now. We got £29.50 a week in the first year. The club also paid our travel expenses and either paid for your digs or gave your parents housekeeping if you still lived at home. I was lucky that my mum used to give me the housekeeping money, but all my mates who had left school were earning much more money than me. I even had a couple of friends who stayed on in the sixth form at Bexley Grammar who got more working a Saturday job than I did playing for Spurs. The first team wasn't on anything like the wages bandied about now but there were still some players earning £6,000 a week. I didn't care and for me the money never came into it. Every day I was blessed to play football as my job. I used to wake up in the morning excited at my day ahead; I couldn't wait to get there. There were also other ways to make money and once a week we used to have to do work experience. The year before I joined, the players still had to do one of their work experiences at a factory. The idea was to show the YTS boys how lucky they were to be footballers and push them to work harder. Our work experience was working in the press office (sitting around chatting to the press officer), coaching a local school in the ball pit and working in the club shop. In the end, they stopped us working in the club shop as the YTS boys were robbing it blind.

As a YTS player you got very little money, and you would actually be jealous of your friends with normal jobs when it came to income. You had to do a few questionable things to supplement that money. The training kits were another thing that would regularly go missing. Each day the youth team kit man, Johnny Wallace, used to drop all the kit into the youth team changing rooms. It would be all wrapped up in a towel. It would then be a mad rush to get the best kits. Towels would be unrolled and you would search through them to find an unused top or a pair of socks that hadn't been washed so many times you couldn't get them above your calves. If you got a brand-new kit, then at the end of training you would put it in your bag and sell it to your mates at home. First team players' boots often went missing too. You could always find a Spurs fan wanting to buy a genuine pair of boots from their idol. Neil Smith used to clean Gary Lineker's boots and he would regularly steal pairs. He used to call it payment for the Christmas bonus Lineker never gave him. When he signed professional forms, Sol Campbell was Neil's boot boy. Neil says that when he saw Sol play, he told him not to bother cleaning his boots any more!

Johnny Wallace was quite a character. He looked a bit like Mr Magoo and had thick bottle-bottom glasses. He had been at the club forever. In the war he had been a medic so at one stage he was the sponge man for the first team. I believe he also took the youth team in the 1960s. His job now was to prepare the kits for training and then take them to and from White Hart Lane and the training ground. A lot of the youth team players used to meet at White Hart Lane and then travel to the training ground on Johnny's minibus. Getting to White Hart Lane was a lot easier than getting to the training ground so most of the youth team went that way. Sometimes you would also have jobs to do at the ground like clean the changing room so you had no choice but to join Johnny. You could tell that Johnny wasn't too impressed by having to take the youth team players. He clearly saw his main job as being the kit man.

The bus would leave at eight in the morning, and I mean at exactly eight. He would sit there with the engine running and watch his clock. Then at exactly eight the doors would close and he would be off. You could have a foot on the step, he didn't care. He would gladly run you over if you tried to stop him. I'm not sure any youth player ever got a word out of Johnny other than 'f*** off'. His other ways of communicating were with grunts and by passing wind, very loudly.

The thing was, we all loved him. What you saw was what you got. It would be like a game, trying to get on the minibus before he drove off, and if you missed it then you knew it was your fault and took it on the chin. We used to try and ring his bell on the bus as many times as we could before he spotted us. We would then shout out the record to see who could ring it the most times without being caught. You would hear cries of 'three's the record' or 'four's the record'. What gave the game an edge was that if Johnny managed to spot you ringing the bell, he would pull over, no matter where he was, and make you leave the bus. You then had to try and make your own way to training. He did not give a f***, and he spoke to everyone at the club in the same way. I once saw a first team player get very annoyed when Johnny told him to f*** off after the player had asked him to take something back to White Hart Lane. Johnny did his job and nothing more, nothing less. The player then complained to Doug Livermore, the assistant manager, who just shrugged and told him that was just Johnny being

My mum and dad got married in 1963. At the time they lived in a flat overlooking the pitch at Highbury. My dad didn't like football at the time.

It's always important to start early!

I am in the back row far left. I was nine and a year younger than the other players when I played for my primary school. Paul Rooke (centre front row) was the captain and recommended me to Villacourt Rovers.

Villacourt Rovers. Standing: Manager Barry Owen
Back row: Lee Botten, Darren Hancock, Stephen Campfield, Danny Owen, Danny Wareham
Front row: Alistair Stuart, Jason Peters, Lee Clarke, Me, Kevin Horlock, Elliot Taylor

The FA Youth Cup quarter-final at Old Trafford. I won man of the match against Manchester United much to the surprise of Kevin Smith.

FA Youth Cup winners. Back row: Ollie Morah, Greg Howell, Warren Hackett, Kevin Smith, David Tuttle, Lee Fulling, Neil Smith.
Front row: Me, Scott Houghton, Ian Walker, Ian Hendon, Vic Hardwicke, Stuart Nethercott.

A photographer took this picture for a local newspaper story about my signing professional forms for Spurs. They wanted an action shot but I was in a leg brace that went from the top of my thigh to my ankle following my knee reconstruction.

Alan Sugar and Terry Venables (right) join forces to buy Tottenham Hotspur Football Club, 22 June 1991. It seemed like the perfect match at the time.

Tottenham Reserves. Back row: Ray Clemence, Ollie Morah, Mark Hall, Stuart Nethercott, David Tuttle, Ian Walker, Ian Hendon, John Cheesewright, Kevin Smith, Peter Garland, David McDonald, Keith Waldon.
Front Row: Neil Smith, Nick Barmby, Me, Greg Howell, Darren Caskey, Jeff Minton, Neil Young, Matt Edwards.

Paul Gascoigne receives medical treatment for his knee injury sustained during the match after a tackle on Nottingham Forest's Gary Charles. John Sheridan and Dave Butler are first on the scene.

Paul Gascoigne in discussion with physio Dave Butler (left) and manager Peter Shreeves as he begins running as part of his rehabilitation following a serious knee injury in the 1991 FA Cup Final. Paul Moran is also in the picture.

Paul Gascoigne in Rome with Glenn Roeder. After Gazza's nightclub incident, Roeder decided not to move to Rome with Gazza and I was asked to take his place.

Me playing for the reserves against Fulham in 1993. This was one of the last games I ever played for Spurs.

Playing non-league football for Tonbridge Angels. My heart was never really in it and I was always battling against injuries.

Johnny, and that Johnny spoke to everyone like that. It was a time when history and tradition still meant something in football and people treated Johnny with respect because of how long he had been a servant to the club. He was allowed to play up because he was part of the club.

When I first joined Spurs, you would still see Bill Nicholson wandering around the club. He was incredibly well respected and all the players were in awe of him. Occasionally, he would pull you over and dig you out for something that he had seen you do in a recent game. No one would argue back, and it felt like an honour to have him even know who you were. Everyone was extremely respectful of him for what he had done for the club. The walls all had pictures of players from Spurs' past and you really felt like part of something bigger. I hope it is still like that, but there is a part of me that suspects it isn't. It's part of why I hate the whole Premier League thing, where anything before 1992 is ignored as if it doesn't count. One of the best things about football is its history and its place in the hearts of generations of fans. Just the other day I heard them talk of Harry Kane as being Spurs' all-time top scorer even though he was still 57 goals short of the great Jimmy Greaves. Stats that ignore what happened before 1992 are disrespectful and only diminish football.

Another way of getting some extra income was through official club merchandise. As a player you could buy stuff in the club shop at cost price. You would take orders off your friends and then add on a bit for your trouble. In my first month as a YTS I paid out £300 of my own savings and travelled the two-hour journey home with two huge bags packed with official merchandise. The problem was, I was exhausted from pre-season training and fell asleep on the train. I woke up just as we pulled into Welling station and scrambled off the train before it started to pull away. Minus the bags! Someone got a lucky break that day.

We also used to get a couple of tickets for the first team games. You could always get a bit of money from the ticket touts outside the ground, who knew you were players. We would often pool our tickets together and one of the more brazen YTS boys would go outside and negotiate a good deal, normally Greg. I'm sure this must disgust any real football fans reading this but we were 16 and 17 years old and desperate for money, although it's probably still no excuse. Some of the more money-grabbing YTS boys would even sell their own ticket and watch the game in the players' lounge on one of the screens. If they were really lucky, one of the executive boxes would be empty and they could watch in luxury!

As well as work experience, we also used to have jobs to do that would change every few weeks. Things like cleaning the footballs, putting them out for training and then collecting them back in at the end. This was a horrible job. You would basically have to take a shower with all the balls to clean them before training started and then carry out five or six big bags of footballs before dropping them at various places out on the fields. You would end up with rope burns on your fingers. The fields were huge, probably the equivalent of about ten football pitches. At the end of training, you would then have to search in bushes and over fences to make sure you returned the same number of footballs as you had brought out.

The first team were the worst. They would kick the balls in all directions at the end of training knowing you had to then go and collect them. In pre-season it was the worst job of the lot. You were exhausted from all the running, and could hardly walk. It would take so long that first team players would have finished training, showered and eaten then drive past in their flash cars beeping their horns at your misfortune. It was also terrible in the winter when your hands would be frozen and the balls would be caked in mud.

One of the other jobs was cleaning the changing rooms after the first team games. I actually enjoyed it because you got to see the other teams as they left following the match. It was like a peep behind the curtain, a nod back to FA Cup Final day. Some of the clothes they wore! I remember John Barnes in a corduroy suit and Jason Cundy wearing cowboy boots that had a huge heel. The only problem was that the rooms were left in an awful state. I couldn't do them justice in any description. The away rooms were always the worst. If Tottenham had won, then you would dread going in there as they would be absolutely trashed. On those occasions it would be seven or eight in the evening before you would get away. Sometimes I would get back home at gone ten after a first team game, and I wouldn't even have the energy to go back out.

You also had to clean the boots of two of the first team squad. I must admit I was terrible at this. You were supposed to scrape the mud off with a wire brush, wash them, dry them, polish them and then buff them up. Finally, you would take them up to the first team changing rooms and leave them on the steps ready for when your pro would turn up. I had David Howells and Paul Moran, and I was lucky they were two of the nicer professionals at the club. They would sometimes laugh as they threw the boots back at me. I deserved it because I used to do a terrible job. Most the time I would just jump to the last part and polish the boots straight over the mud. I can remember Paul coming down to the boot room one morning and slaughtering me in front of everyone. He was actually picking the polished mud off his boots in clumps. It was all done in fun, but I was mortified and did try to do a better job afterwards. I suffered at Christmas, though, because while other players gave out decent bonuses to their boot boys, David and Paul, quite rightly, kept their money in their pockets. Ollie Morah was very lucky as he did Gazza's boots. At Christmas, Gazza just chucked a wad of money. It was just loose money from in his pockets, but it was a small fortune. I don't think I ever saw Ollie so happy; he loved a pound note.

As a first-year YTS boy, you were the lowest of the low. The other players treated you poorly as did the coaching staff. The staff offices were upstairs and overlooked the training pitches. You had to walk right under the window if you wanted to get a drink or something to eat. The first-years used to try and get past without being noticed. If you were spotted, you would be sent off to get teas for all the coaches. That wasn't the worst bit though. The minute you entered the office they would all start, ripping you to pieces over aspects of your game or even the way you looked. It was brutal. Sometimes you would be stuck there for 20 minutes just listening to how bad you ran the day before, or how you were too scruffy or dissecting a bad moment in your last game.

Ultimately, I think I was lucky that I was at Spurs. They were a big club and did look after their young players. Some of the stories I heard from other clubs were nothing more than bullying. You had to stick up for yourself or you could end up a victim. I remember reading a piece from Gary Neville and some of the things they had to put up with at Manchester United sounded awful. Things like young players being put into the clothes dryer and it being turned on, or being stripped naked and sent out in the snow to run around the training field. Gary felt that it helped them in the end, and built their character. These days, there is quite rightly a lot of concern over people's mental health and looking back I am sure that it damaged some people. Nonetheless, it was character-building and it did separate the wheat from the chaff, though at what cost I am not sure. I do think that now young players get too much too soon and can lack mental toughness, so maybe it has gone too far the other way.

We also had to go to college once a week. We would have a tutor who would come into the ground and teach us. It was a City and Guilds course in Sport and Recreation and it was painfully easy. It is often levied at footballers that they are thick. I was never a great student, but I did leave school with six GCSEs, which made me Einstein in the world of football. It used to amaze me that the other YTS boys could understand complex tactics and formations but could not answer the most basic question. It was painful. The tutor would ask something like what would you have to consider before carrying a heavy piece of equipment. The answers were so obvious; is it too heavy to lift, will it fit through the door, do you need to go upstairs, will you need more than one person and so on. I used to be itching to answer but didn't want to set myself apart from the rest of the team. One YTS boy, Steven Bence, was very academic and he soon separated himself from the herd with his in-depth answers. The poor tutor must have hated 'teaching' us.

You always needed to make sure that you were one of the lads. It was a real mob mentality. Fitting in was so important and conformity was everything. Players who stood out could have a really hard time of it. Gary Mabbutt was the perfect professional but because he didn't go out drinking with the other players and wasn't married, you would hear the players gossiping about him. It was ridiculous but there was so much pressure to fit in. You felt like you needed to wear the same clothes and like the same music as everyone else. There were lots of stories in football of players who lived different lifestyles and were ostracised from the team. When a player like Gary got targeted you knew that it had gone crazy.

The intake for the youth team in my year was a light one for players. We had John Cheesewright in goal, with Stuart Nethercott, Steven Bence and Neil Young in defence. Greg Howell and Mark Hall were in midfield and it was me and Ollie up front. It was soon down to seven players as Steven quit for America. It was probably for the best he was well educated and well spoken; he was clearly going to find life as a professional footballer very tough.

My very first training session as a YTS player really brought home the competitive environment I was now part of. We did a beep test: a 20-metre run that you start at one beep and have to finish by the time of the next beep. As the test progresses the gap between beeps shortens until you are having to sprint to get there on time. It is a test designed to measure your fitness and is not a pleasant experience. As you get more tired you have to get quicker, which is not a good combination.

There was a moment in this run when everyone had the realisation that they couldn't be the first person to drop out. Unlike Gary Lineker, we did not have a reputation built up over hundreds of games and hundreds of goals to fall back on. We were in direct competition with each other. There were 30

YTS boys doing that run, and at most seven or eight would get a professional contract. That first run, on that first day was a microcosm of our situation. Look to your left and look to your right, if they beat you then they can take away your dream. I was acutely aware that this was a competition and was not going to drop out unless my legs could no longer move. The problem was that everyone else had the same thought. It was torture.

And so pre-season continued. Every session was a battle with yourself to push yourself to your very limit. You felt like everything you did was being judged and you could never relax. Every day was excruciating. Plus, of course, you *were* being judged. Everything you did could make the difference between making it or not. Have a bad time in your running and you could be labelled as lazy. Look annoyed when you get subbed and you have a bad attitude. Come off like you don't care, then you don't want it enough. Don't fly into a tackle, you are a coward. Jump into tackles, you have no discipline. Sometimes you felt like you couldn't win.

One of the runs we did in pre-season was where you were organised into groups of ten or 12 and you were put with a partner. You then made a line of pairs. Your group went jogging all around the field staying in a line. When the whistle was blown the back two had to sprint to the front, when they got there the next two had to sprint and so on. You kept sprinting from back to front until the whistle was blown. It went on for ages and was really tough. What made it tougher was the fact that all the players took part, so in your group you would have people from the youth team, reserves and first team. The first team players would all be on at the youth team lads to slow down. These were seasoned pros who had been there and done it. They didn't want over-enthusiastic youngsters making them look bad. You couldn't win because your coaches would be watching you and making judgements, but peer pressure was huge and the first team players could feel very intimidating.

About the third time of doing this I was put in the same group as Terry Fenwick. Terry was Terry Venables's first signing for Spurs. He knew Terry's character and footballing knowledge. When Terry played, he used to run the whole defensive game for Spurs, organising when to push up and when to drop. The team always played better with him on the pitch. At one point in his Spurs career he became a target of the Tottenham boo boys, who didn't realise how important he was. But you wouldn't know unless you were privy to what was happening behind the scenes.

In one game, the East Stand was closed for repairs and Terry scored. He celebrated in front of the empty stand in a clear dig at the fans who had been giving him stick. He wasn't the most talented player, but he got by on football smarts. I played in a reserve game with him once. Well, I was a substitute. Scott Houghton was on the wing and had just easily beaten his defender. Ray Clemence on the bench told me to watch what Terry did. Sure enough, the next four or five times Terry got the ball he popped it straight off to Scott. We scored two goals through Scott roasting his full-back that day. I also learned a valuable lesson in being a professional, and playing with intelligence.

Back to the running that day in pre-season, and Terry organised our whole group. As we did the first jog, before the whistle blew, he told us that when we ran we had to give it lots of arms and faces. What he meant was to pump your arms and put a grimace on your face. No one would notice that your legs weren't moving too quickly. He would also make sure that the two who ran from the back stopped straight away when they got to the front. Otherwise, the gap from back to front would get longer, therefore so too would the sprint. I always tried to get on his team after that. Even in five-a-side he would have his team so organised that they would always win. Venables ended up earmarking him as his replacement, but it never quite happened. Terry has gone on to have a very successful career managing abroad in Trinidad and Tobago. I always thought that management of Spurs should have come out and explained why he was so important to the team when the stick was at its worst. Most football fans would appreciate being let in on his strengths, and it may have eased the abuse.

A week into pre-season there was a train strike, and I had to stay with Ian Walker in digs for a couple of nights. I dreaded it because nutrition and diet are very important for a footballer and frankly my diet was shocking. I ate meat, potatoes and chocolate – nothing else! I knew that the lady who ran the digs would be preparing proper meals that I wouldn't like, and I was scared it would get reported back to Spurs. In the end I managed to force down a bit of the meal and then claimed that I was a small eater and was full. Later, I snuck out and bought some chips from the local chippy.

On the first morning I was there, I literally crawled down the stairs for breakfast. Every part of me ached from pre-season training and I didn't know how I was going to get through that day's session. After breakfast, I needed to use the bathroom. I remember standing at the bottom of the stairs knowing I couldn't make it up them. I had to sneak into the garden and relieve myself behind a bush!

The next night, me and Walks went out for a few games of pool at a nearby pub. As we walked, we passed a few pubs with pool tables in them. Curious, I asked why we didn't go in them. Walks told me the club had people who they sent around the local pubs to make sure that the players in digs were tucked up at home and not out drinking. Walks had fallen foul a couple of times so now had to go a little further out to avoid them.

Ian was a one-off. In my whole time at the club, he was always laughing and joking. He didn't seem to take anything too seriously, except for his football. I notice on Tottenham Hotspur forums that he is still someone who splits opinion. When you delve deeper, the people who criticise him seem to concentrate more on his hair than his goalkeeping. The other criticism aimed at him is the Gianfranco Zola goal at Wembley when England lost 1-0 in a 1998 World Cup qualifier. In writing this I have looked again at the footage, and the ball takes a huge deflection that diverts it over his dive, so I really don't think the goal was Ian's fault at all.

All I can talk about is my time playing with and watching him play at Spurs. He was an incredible goalkeeper; he was the best player in our team that first year. Terry Venables was a massive fan. He earmarked Walks for a first team place even when he was in the youth team. Erik Thorstvedt was a very capable keeper but it was no secret at the club that Ian, at 17, was already technically better and that it would only be a matter of time before he became the number-one choice. The club were aware of Erik's weaknesses and Ray Clemence used to often keep him out after training to work on his game. I used to dread seeing Ray calling Erik over for some extra practice. I knew what was next. 'Pottsy and Ollie get over here,' would come the call. We would then have to challenge Erik as Ray delivered cross after cross. Eric used to smash the hell out of me and Ollie as he came to claim the cross. He was huge and built like a brick outhouse, and I would have bruises on bruises after every extra session with him. Me and Ollie used to try and sneak off before Ray saw us but he always caught us or sent someone to find us.

In training, Ian was also a nightmare for me. As a forward, you want to get a few goals during the week to get in a groove for the game at the weekend. I would sometimes go weeks without managing to beat him; no matter what I did he always found a way to make the save. In the end it was another thing that helped improve me as I had to make sure my finishing was always spot on, even in training. When we had shooting practice it was normally a cue for all sorts of outrageous goals, but with Walks in goal it was different. He used to start counting after his first save. 'One' then 'two' then 'three' and so on. It would be so annoying as he reached a stupidly high number of saves before anyone finally beat him. He played at Spurs for 12 years and I genuinely don't think he gets the respect he deserves.

Keith Waldon came up to me and Ollie Morah very early in pre-season and told us that there was a spot for us in the South East Counties Division One team if we linked up well in pre-season. He told us that they had not brought in a replacement for Neil Carey as they felt we could both step up. The plan was for one of us to play but Keith felt that if we played well as a pair, we could both make the team. For me, that was all I needed to hear.

Ollie was big and quick and always looking to run in behind. I knew this would suit my game as I could then play a little deeper than him and then look to put him in on goal. Every time we played a game in training, I would look to get the ball to Ollie at every opportunity. As I got used to the runs he made, we started to develop a bit of an understanding. It didn't go unnoticed, and in the first friendly we were both in the squad for the A team. That friendly was memorable for being the most tired I have ever been during a game of football. The youth team that year was full of big personalities, who would go on to have long careers and then become managers and coaches. Our keeper and back four were Ian Walker, Ian Hendon, Neil Smith, Warren Hackett and David Tuttle. They all had long careers in league football and all went on to manage and coach. Our backup defender was a first-year YTS player like me, Stuart Nethercott, who again had a long career before going into coaching and management. Even the backup full-back, Neil Young, went on to have a long career and moved into coaching. That's about 3,000 league appearances with those seven players alone.

On the pitch, they were incredibly demanding of you. At one point about 20 minutes into the game, I remember sharing a look with Ollie. We didn't have enough breath to talk so it was a look of despair. We both didn't think we were going to be able to get through the game. We never got a moment's peace, constantly being directed on where to go and what to do. But we did get through and we went on to play pretty much every game that year finishing as the top two scorers in the South East Counties League – just above Andy Cole at Arsenal. I was very proud to finish as the top scorer with 22 goals, as scoring was no longer the currency I measured my performances in. My main job was linking up the play and to provide assists. The fact that I also managed to score a few was a bonus really.

Our midfield that year was bossed by Kevin Smith, and in fact the whole team probably was. Kevin never had the career that his talent deserved. By his own admission he was never the most professional, but among a team of personalities his was the strongest. He improved me as a player and person more in that year than any of my coaches. He was on my back from minute one, and sometimes I wanted to scream at him to shut up. But he scared the life out of me and was normally right. I also knew it came from a good place and if he didn't rate or like me, he wouldn't have bothered. He was a Roy Keane type of a player but with more ability, I kid you not. Neil Smith and him were very close friends and Neil always said that Kevin was either going to be something spectacular, the best of a generation, or do what he did and drift out of the game. He tragically died young, and I often think of him.

Alongside Kevin was normally Vic Hardwick, but Greg Howell played a lot of games too and probably offered us a little more when he did play. We had two good wingers in Lee Fulling and Scott Houghton. Scott also went on to have a long career, but he was crazy. Completely mad. He was small in stature but incredibly strong; I once saw him bench press every weight on the machine at Spurs. He was also very quick and scored a lot of goals. But he had a temper! He could fly off the handle at the slightest provocation and everyone had a funny story involving Scott. I can remember him once headbutting his marker while dribbling the ball past him at Bournemouth. I still don't know how he did it.

The first team had a decent season that year, although the squad wasn't very deep. Man for man, it was far inferior to the side of two years previous. They were very reliant on a few key players that year: Gary Mabbutt at the back, Gary Lineker up front and Paul Gascoigne in midfield. There was very little squad rotation and in reality it was a 14-man squad for the majority of the season with only injuries or suspensions changing the starting 11. Steve Sedgley and Pat Van Den Hauwe were brought in to add a bit of steel and defensive know-how because Terry Fenwick ended up breaking his leg and missed the majority of the season. Chris Hughton was seeing out his final campaign and only played eight league games.

Already you could see a policy of bringing in players with reputations for being difficult to manage, relying on Terry Venables to get a tune out of them. That way Spurs could pay below the players' real market value as other clubs just wanted them out. A lot of accusations have been made of Venables over the years but man-management has always been one of his many strengths. For example, Paul Walsh and Pat Van Den Hauwe were excellent players but both of them came with their own demons. Paul was considered the most talented player at an incredibly talented Liverpool in his time there, but he went off the rails. I have seen recently him admit that he had a spell in his career where he let himself down with his drinking and lifestyle. I loved him as a player as he was another in the Dalglish mould. I had followed his career since he started at

Charlton Athletic. He lived in Plumstead, down the road from where I grew up in Welling. I had always thought that he could have been one of the best players produced by England, but he never quite got there. I felt sorry for him at Spurs as he was always considered a backup player. I even remember him scoring a great hat-trick when Paul Stewart was suspended and he still got dropped for the next game. Walshy had a short fuse and I remember at one reserve game I came on for him, and him and Ray Clemence nearly came to blows about him being substituted. I was also there at a first team game when he was an unused substitute. Straight after the game, the subs had to run laps of the pitch to keep their fitness up. It was like the ultimate insult; you don't play, then you have to run. You could see he was already annoyed. Then someone in the crowd gave him a bit of abuse. Before you knew it, Paul was up over the fence and trying to fight the fan, who was suddenly not as brave as he previously was.

Pat was another thing altogether. I recently read his book, and how he was able to perform at the level he did with what was going on with him outside football I will never know. Secretly, the YTS team referred to him as 'Mad Pat' as he always looked like he was about to kick off. In a game, he was a snarling ball of anger, and I genuinely used to feel sorry for his opponent. Before the players went out, the referee used to come in to check their studs. Once the referee left, David Butler, the first team physio, would go and get Pat's real boots along with their filed-down metal studs! In the changing room before a game, he would prowl around like a caged animal.

We once played Derby, and Ted McMinn started to give some verbals to Pat. I can still remember all the YTS boys sharing a look, and Greg Howell remarking that you don't want to be doing that to Mad Pat. Sure enough, ten minutes later McMinn was stretchered off. At half-time Pat had to be held back from trying to get in the physio room to finish what he started. McMinn was never the same player again. When I finally got to play and train with Pat, I saw a completely different side to him. He had won league titles at Everton, even scoring the goal that won the First Division one year, and yet he would go out of his way to make sure you were okay and spoke to everyone from YTS first-year players to Terry Venables as equals.

There were times that season when Venables must have felt like he was juggling and trying to keep all the balls in the air. Along with Walsh and Van Den Hauwe, Paul Gascoigne needed constant man-managing. He was outstanding that year and won the Spurs' player of the year award, despite Gary Lineker being the league's top scorer. But off the pitch he was always up to something. There was never a week without a story of something he had got up to. Even then he was a drinker, but so were most of the squad. Some of the older professionals like Gary Mabbutt, Chris Hughton and Paul Allen stood out for their professionalism and, must have despaired at some of the things that were going on. In reality though, the drinking culture was what really brought that team together. They were friends *and* team-mates. On the pitch, they gave everything for the shirt.

That team lost three and drew one of their first five league games and yet still managed to finish the season in third place, above Arsenal. How Venables held the team together I will never know. There were clear gaps in the squad. They desperately needed another centre-half to play alongside Mabbutt, and they only had Paul Allen who was a natural wide player. Players like Steve Sedgley, Mitchell Thomas, David Howells and Gudni Bergsson played all over the place filling in for the gaps in the squad. Can you imagine a Premier League team now just using the same 14 players all year?

My favourite part of training would be a Friday where the youth team squad was drafted in for matchday preparations. We would be given the parts of the opposition players at the weekend. For example, if we were playing Liverpool then Ollie would be John Aldridge and I would be Peter Beardsley. Venables would set up free kicks, throw-ins and corners and direct us to where our chosen player would normally be. It was all based on hours of scouting of the opposition. It was fascinating stuff. He would say things to me like, 'Right Pottsy, Beardsley starts off here than at the last moment he makes this sort of run,' and he would then show me. He would go around all of us doing this and although there was a lot of standing around, no one complained, not even the first team players. Everyone could see the quality and importance of what he was doing. His level of expertise and eye for detail were second to none. After we had run through the set piece a couple of times, he would then coach the first team players on how to nullify what their opponents were doing. You could tell that the first team players held him in high esteem and they would follow his instructions to the letter. He was so clear and concise and after about an hour of this the improvement would be obvious. It would then be great to watch the game and see the things he had coached being put into practice.

Venables was an amazing coach and had probably forgotten more than most others will ever know. There were times in these sessions that, as he walked past me, he would offer me bits of advice; this when he was supposed to be working on the first team's set pieces. I can remember one time I seemed to be giving the ball away a lot in the last game against Chelsea, and often Frank Sinclair kept getting in front of me and getting possession. I was getting frustrated and so were the other players, especially Kevin Smith. In the Friday session, Venables noticed that the angle I was coming off my defender was too straight so I couldn't see the defender coming. He hadn't known about the Chelsea game and my frustrations; he had just noticed it in passing. In our game the following day I didn't give the ball away once.

Venables's advice was always spot on and I never needed to ask for it, he would just spot something within what he was doing. There was always that dodgy Tel side that you would hear about though. One of the coaching staff once told us that Venables had been involved in a suspect pension scheme at one of the clubs he had played at. A lot of players lost money through it. The press were always speculating about his suspect business deals. Whether that was true or not it was a label that stuck and ultimately it was to cause his demise at Spurs.

That season I travelled in to training with Kevin and Neil Smith. Sometimes we would meet Warren Hackett and Scott Houghton on the way. They were all second-year YTS lads, and it could be a bit intimidating. This was at a time when the second-year YTS players ruled the roost over the first-year players and you were forced to just take whatever sh** they threw at you. It was like a rite of passage. I was well outnumbered on the journeys so used to listen more than I spoke, but they were funny times. Neil Smith, in particular, tells a great story and my sides would ache from laughter by the time I got to training.

It was a long journey. We had to get the train into London Bridge and then a tube to the end of the Northern Line, literally the end of the line. Once we got to Mill Hill East it was either a 30-minute walk or a bus. The problem was the bus only came once every half-hour and it was too risky to wait in case you had just missed one, so more often than not we would end up walking. One time, as we got off the tube at Mill Hill East, Scott was off. He never said a word but he sprinted down the platform, leapt the ticket machine and flew down the stairs.

We soon realised what had happened; he had spotted the bus coming up the road through the train carriage window. We soon set off after him, but we were too late; the doors had closed and it started to pull away. There was Scott on the top floor mooning us all out the back window. From that angle he couldn't see what we could see. He had got on the wrong bus. We all kept our best disappointed looks on our faces while we watched him disappear off around the corner in the wrong direction. He ended up being late for training and got a telling off from Keith Waldon, which just made it better.

Another time Kevin got in a big argument with an Arsenal fan who had seen us in our Spurs tracksuits. The discussion continued as we boarded our train and Kevin was leaning out the window giving the Gunner dog's abuse. The supporter began to run down the platform giving it back to Kevin. Then BANG! He ran straight into a sign on the platform, which knocked him flat on his backside. It was like a scene from a Laurel and Hardy movie. That was it, we were now all at the window giving it to him as he wiped the blood from his nose.

On the pitch things couldn't have gone any better. Although I scored 22 goals in the league that year, I actually managed to score 30 goals in 45 matches overall. We won three trophies. The first came in the South East Counties Junior Floodlit Cup. I don't think they could fit the full title on the trophy, it was so long, but it was a great competition to play in. The league games were all played at teams' training grounds on a Saturday morning, but as the name suggests this cup was all played under floodlights at the actual grounds. We played at Bournemouth in the first round. Jamie Redknapp played and was amazing despite the fact we beat them 6-0. Next up were Wimbledon, who did the full Crazy Gang treatment on us, flooding the changing room and taking the plug off the heater. The tie ended up going to penalties before we finally saw them off. After that came a comfortable win against Leyton Orient, before we met Watford in the semi-final. Watford were a very strong side having won the FA Youth Cup the year before. David James was in goal and the two games were a lot more even than the score suggests. In the end, we managed to beat them 5-2 on aggregate putting us through to the final, where we played Arsenal.

That year, we were a mentally and physically strong team that was full of leaders. Don't get me wrong, we played good football as that was the Tottenham way, but it was our mental strength that stood us apart. Arsenal, though, were probably a better team. In the league they had beaten us comfortably with Andy Cole unplayable. Playing Arsenal was always a huge game for Tottenham. That year we all watched the two reserve sides play in what can only be described as a war. There were five players sent off and there were some of the worst challenges I had ever seen on a football pitch. I can remember one from Brian Statham that should have come with a parental warning. It did show us how important any game versus our neighbours from north London was.

In the first leg at White Hart Lane, we lost 1-0. Scott Houghton was sent off and we spent the whole game on the back foot. Ian Walker was outstanding, and we were fortunate to only be losing by one goal at the finish. You could tell that they thought they had done enough. There was a certain arrogance at the final whistle, and it didn't go unnoticed. Between the first and second legs we were to get a little help. John Lyall had been a legendary manager at West Ham, winning two FA Cups and building one of their greatest teams as they won promotion from the Second Division. He then built another team, which ended up recording a club record position of third in the First Division. He was out of management at the time and Terry Venables had asked him to come along to training to put on a few sessions.

Other than Venables himself, John was probably the best coach I had ever seen. His sessions were great fun and we used to look forward to seeing what he had in store for us as they were always so imaginative. In the time between the first leg and second leg, John went to watch the Arsenal youth team play. He spotted a weakness on the left of their defence, and we worked all week on getting Ollie across on that side, one on one. In the first ten minutes of the second leg our plan worked like a dream. Twice Ollie latched on to a diagonal pass to score exactly the sort of goal we had been practising all week. John had also worked on a defensive shape to nullify the talented Gunners team. It wasn't a very enjoyable game for me as I had to sacrifice my attacking play and play almost like a left-winger. My job was to stop the full-back getting forward and help out our actual winger. But it worked. We were never really in danger, except late into the second half when Arsenal had a corner in front of the North Bank. As the taker started his run-up, I had a fleeting vision of me volleying it into the back of the net, scoring the winning goal for Arsenal in front of where I used to stand a few years previously. I was honestly tempted. In the end, I volleyed the ball clear and we hung on to win a well-earned victory. John left to manage Ipswich Town, and I went back up front.

In the second half of the season, it became clear we were going to secure a sixth straight league title, and we began to focus on the FA Youth Cup, a very prestigious trophy. I could remember Pat Holland telling us it was one of his biggest regrets to never have won it. In your whole career you only really got two chances to win it, in your two years as a YTS player. We had made our way through to the quarter-finals without too much difficulty, beating Wolverhampton Wanderers and Colchester United, but then we were up against Manchester City at Maine Road. City were known to have one of the best youth systems in the country at that time. They had got to the final the year before and won it three years prior to that.

We travelled the day before and stayed in a hotel in Manchester, preparing exactly as the first team would have done. I felt like a real player and it made me even more determined to make the most of my opportunity. Thankfully, dinner was chicken, which I could eat, and we had tea and toast before departing for the game in the evening. It was one of those nights where everything just felt right. The preparation was spot on and even in the warm-up it felt good. We had expected another close match, but instead we put on our best performance of the season and the 2-0 score was flattering to City. I felt it was my best performance of the season, and at the time Keith Waldon said that he felt I was man of the match.

The semi-final brought another tie with a Manchester side as we were drawn against Manchester United. In goal they had Mark Bosnich and in the centre of midfield was Alex Ferguson's son Darren. Our scouting report told us that they had two very quick, very skilful wingers. It was right. On one wing was Ryan Giggs, at the time called Ryan Wilson, and on the other they had a lad called Adrian Doherty, who was considered an even better prospect than Ryan. This is something that Ryan readily admits. Adrian was a skilful winger from Northern Ireland, so the George Best comparisons were obvious. Unfortunately, his career followed a similar pattern to mine. He tore his cruciate ligament but tried to manage it rather than have an operation. Eventually he was forced to go under the knife but was never the same. He gave up football at the age of 20, then at the age of 26 he was found unconscious in a canal in The Hague and spent a month in a coma before dying. His death was ruled accidental. It was a tragic loss.

Ferguson had only been at United for a few seasons and one of his goals was to improve the youth system. That was to prove very successful, as history will certify. People at the club say that he was obsessed with winning the FA Youth Cup. In Manchester United's history, the FA Youth Cup had signalled great things for the club, from the Busby Babes to the unearthing of Best. However, it was just over 25 years since their last success, when their team including Best won 5-2 against Sunderland in 1964. This year, Ferguson felt it was their year and he was expecting them to win. We went into the semi-final as massive underdogs.

They were a very strong team but so were we. In the first leg at White Hart Lane we steamrollered them. We won 2-0 but it could have been more. Ryan Giggs was up against Warren Hackett, and Warren scared the life out of him. He was in Giggs's ear the whole game and snapping at his heels throughout. Giggs went missing and psychologically it was a big thing in the context of the game. The away end was nearly full. United brought huge support along for the game, clearly expecting to see a victory. You could tell that their players' pride had been wounded. Their attitudes had not been right and they had turned up certain they were going to win. I don't think they expected us to be as good as we were. We knew that it wasn't over as the Arsenal game had shown us the dangers of complacency, and we knew the second leg was going to prove a lot more difficult.

The second leg was at Old Trafford, and it was the polar opposite of the first. In front of a big crowd we were on the back foot for the whole game. Giggs was ready for Warren, and he looked a different player, while Doherty was causing us lots of problems on the other wing. It was Doherty who scored an early goal and one more would have brought them level on aggregate. How we didn't concede a second I will never know. Great defending and some missed chances meant that with about five minutes to go the score remained at 1-0. Then, following an onslaught of United attacks, the ball found me just outside the United area. In truth, I had not had the best of games. I had given the ball away too often, when I could have relieved some of the pressure on the team by holding it up. Kevin Smith was on my back and it was not an enjoyable night. This was one of those cases where confidence was so important. It would have been easy to just play a safe pass, but I saw a bit of a gap and was able to dribble past a couple of players and get through on goal. Bosnich came out and I shot across him. I couldn't honestly say if the ball was going in or not but luckily Lee Fulling had been alert and slid in at the far post to make sure. We were through to the final. The supporters gave me a bottle of champagne for the man of the match award, and I tried to avoid Kevin's gaze as they handed it over in the bar after.

Middlesbrough had beaten Portsmouth in the other semi-final so we travelled to Ayresome Park for the first leg of the final. It felt a little bit like after the Lord Mayor's Show, as we had knocked out the two favourites in the previous rounds and we felt very confident going into the final. The kick-off was delayed due to there being a bigger crowd than expected. We were always on top and Scott Houghton gave us the lead with a fine finish after a great move. Middlesbrough equalised against the run of play, but in the second half a great ball by Kevin put me through on goal slightly to the right. I took the shot early and it fizzed into the far corner to give us a 2-1 lead to take into the second leg. The goal was shown on *Football Focus* and introduced by Bob Wilson. I felt like a million dollars.

The second leg at White Hart Lane was a memorable day, even if the game was a bit of an anticlimax. We scored an early goal through an Ollie Morah header from my cross and then controlled the match, never really looking in danger of letting our advantage slip. I even hit the crossbar with a chip in the second half, nearly adding to our lead. Even when Middlesbrough managed to grab an equaliser on the night, there were never any moments of real danger. It was a fitting end to a great season as we lifted the FA Youth Cup at White Hart Lane in front of our own fans.

Keith Waldon did a great job that year, and I will be forever thankful for the trust he showed in me. It was difficult for Keith. His background was as a teacher, and he had shown himself to be an excellent coach. He went a long way in the game for someone with no real footballing background and pedigree. There is a lot of snobbery in football against people who have not played at the very highest level. People like Keith helped pave the way for others to follow and thankfully football isn't quite as closed a shop as it used to be. I know he managed me well throughout that season, and really got the best out of me, so I have fond memories of him. I was pleased for him when he managed to get the Portsmouth manager's job at one point, ironically after Terry Fenwick was sacked. He was only caretaker for three games but it was still quite an achievement.

I say it was the climax to the season, but that isn't entirely true. There was to be a very significant moment in my career right at the end. Looking back, as I write this book, it was more significant than I ever realised at the time.

The campaign was over and I was looking at potential holiday destinations when my mum called me into the kitchen. She had a letter in her hand. I could see the FA stamp on the front and was instantly intrigued. When I opened up the letter, it was informing me that I had been called up to the shadow squad for the England youth team. The game was at Wembley against France and was going to be before the full England team played against Uruguay in one of two warm-up games before the World Cup finals in Italy. I didn't care that I was only in the shadow squad, when I thought about how it was only a few years beforehand that I hadn't even got through the first round of the trials for Lilleshall. Greg Howell had also made the shadow squad and we were walking on air. Imagine my excitement when I was then called up to the full squad.

9

Three Lions

I CAN remember arriving at Lancaster Gate in London dressed in a newly bought suit to report for England duty. I knew some of the squad and those I hadn't met I knew of by reputation. Ollie Morah from Spurs was also called up and Jamie Redknapp and Darren Hancock were both in too; three of my best friends in football at the time. By now, me and Ollie were very good friends as we had a shared connection from being the only two first-year YTS boys to play all season in the South East Counties Division One side. Ollie was a bit like Sol Campbell in the fact that he was so laid-back. I sometimes used to wonder if he even enjoyed playing football as he never seemed to get too excited over anything. Ollie was very quiet but had a dark sense of humour, and the only time he seemed to get animated was when the insults started flying. He loved the banter at a football club and was always at the centre of it. We were rarely apart that first year.

Ollie's best friend before coming to Spurs was Mark Hall and as a result the three of us spent a lot of time together. Ollie had been at Lilleshall, so he was catching up with a lot of old friends. I felt a little awkward with Darren as he was the best of friends with a lot of the team having spent two years at Lilleshall with them. The Lilleshall boys all had a very tight bond. You could understand why, because they spent every second together from the minute they got up to when they fell asleep at night. It was great to see Darren and catch up a bit but I felt like an outsider. I ended up chatting to and standing with Jamie Redknapp, as it felt like we were the only players there who had not been to Lilleshall. A few of the players had already played first team football, Garry Flitcroft at Manchester City and Lee Clark at Newcastle being two examples. I sat with Jamie on the journey. He had already been getting a lot of attention from his performances with Bournemouth and there was talk of Kenny Dalglish wanting to sign him for Liverpool even then.

We went from Lancaster Gate to a hotel near Bisham Abbey. I don't remember too much about the hotel as my memories are dominated by the training sessions. On the first day, we had a meeting before training. I also can't remember the name of the manager but the talk he gave was awful! I was used to Pat Holland, Keith Waldon and Terry Venables, but this did not live up to what I had experienced up to then. At the time, the FA were obsessed with a book written by one of their own, Charlie Hughes. He had done a study and found that

128

most goals were scored from moves of three passes or fewer. He took this fact and built a whole philosophy based on getting the ball forward as quickly and as often as possible. It is a great example of why statistics can be so dangerous. Yes, a lot of goals came from three or fewer passes but you need to look at what else happens in a match. For example, if you play a fast, short passing game then you bring teams forward on to you, and you can then hit a longer pass to take advantage. I emphasise pass, as Glenn Hoddle was the master of the longer pass but he picked his moments. If all you do is hit it long then the other team are ready for you and it isn't effective. The whole team talk went something like this: 'You have to bloody pass it bloody long and if you don't bloody pass it bloody long then you won't bloody stay on the bloody pitch.' It left me cold.

In training, we practised team shape and it soon became obvious that I would be starting with Ollie up front. The best player in training every day was Jamie Redknapp, who was head and shoulders above the other players. Garry Flitcroft spent the three days trying to kick Jamie as he clearly saw him as a rival. After the first day of training, we knew that Jamie was going to be on the bench. He didn't suit the style of play that England wanted, which in itself was a travesty. I could sympathise with him because, although I was in the team, I knew it didn't suit me either.

We would finish training about midday, and then sit and watch the first team train before we went back to the hotel. I was completely star-struck. Just watching Paul Gascoigne and John Barnes playing one on one for a bit of fun before training was enough for me. I could have sat there all day. Then Stuart Pearce started practising free kicks. He was bending them in from about 25 yards, but still hitting them harder than I had ever seen a ball hit before. One shot hit the crossbar and flew back over his head, nearly landing on the halfway line. Being around all of this really was *Roy of the Rovers* stuff. I just spent the days walking around in a daze, like it was happening to someone else. I felt so close to my dreams that I could reach out and touch them.

On the day before the game, near the end of the last training session, the ball was crossed to the far post. Normally in training I would have just left it as it was a little high. But this was England and I wasn't leaving anything. I just about reached the ball but couldn't control the header, and it went just wide. Then CRUNCH! I landed on the side of my foot and I felt my ankle roll under me. I collapsed to the floor. I had always had slightly weak ankles and would often turn them. Normally I could just run the pain off, but occasionally it would be a bit worse and I might miss a couple of days while I waited for the swelling to go down. The England physio rushed over and got me to stand up and test it. I gingerly walked up and down, which was a good sign, but I couldn't run. I took off my boot and sock and my heart dropped. My ankle had already started to swell up. I felt like crying. I spent the last bit of the session sitting with ice on my ankle. The physio confirmed what I already knew, that if it was still swollen in the morning then I wouldn't be able to play.

When we got back to the hotel, I went straight to my room and kept my ankle iced. I was sharing with Jamie, and that evening he kept a constant stream of ice coming from the machine down the hallway. It was definitely improving but not fast enough. Eventually we had to get some sleep or we would have been no good for the game, bad ankle or no bad ankle. When I got up in the morning, I could walk on my leg but when I tried to jog up and down the hallway it was still painful. There was still a bit of swelling and I knew what the verdict was going to be. Tottenham would have been fuming if England had played me knowing that I was injured. The physio came in with the manager to check on me. Although I already knew what he was going to tell me, it didn't lessen the blow. They told me I could go home or take my place on the bench and do the warm-up. I was still hoping for a miracle so there was never a question of going home. The worst part was having to phone family to say that I wasn't going to be playing. It was a tough phone call and I didn't want to say the words out loud. I can remember fighting back the tears as I spoke on the phone. Everyone was very good and told me to enjoy the day as I was still lucky to just be there. I knew they were right so I made sure that I treated it the same as any other game.

By the time we got on the coach I was walking pretty much normally. I still had hopes that if I could do the warm-up properly then the coaches might see me, and bring me on for part of the game. Even with everything going on in my head, when we got closer to Wembley and I could see the twin towers come into view I became overcome with emotion and I felt a huge surge of pride. It took me back to those FA Cup finals when I was a kid, and I could imagine the teams taking the same journey with the television cameras on the coach beaming it live back to *Saint and Greavsie*. As a kid, there are moments you dream of; playing at Wembley is one of them, as is pulling on the three lions. I knew I probably wouldn't be playing but I still felt a huge feeling of achievement.

We got changed in the huge bathroom as all the first team kits were already laid out in the changing room, ready for their game against Uruguay. The fan in me came flooding out as I walked around the empty changing room imagining what it would be like at 2pm as the players started to get changed. I managed to complete the warm-up even though I probably shouldn't have. It felt great just being out there wearing the kit, kicking a ball on the sacred turf. When the warm-up finished and the 'bloody' team talk was done, I took my place on the bench. I could see a few of the Spurs coaches behind us, and Pat Holland came down the front to offer his commiserations on my injury. It was kind of ironic. I had always suffered with injuries as a kid, but had not missed a single game that season. It was like my luck had finally run out.

Little did I know.

The game itself was something else. The French team were on a different level. There was one player in the centre of the park who ran the show. He was six foot plus and never gave the ball away all game. Every now and then he would burst forward from midfield leaving players floundering behind him. With about ten minutes left I was sent to warm up, but by then my ankle had stiffened up. I came that close to sharing the pitch with Zinedine Zidane. I still count him as the most famous player I ever played against!

English football had been in the doldrums for a while. People remember Bobby Robson very fondly from the 1990 World Cup, but he hadn't enjoyed the smoothest journey as manager. In 1988 at the European Championship, England lost every game and there were calls for his head. The road to Italy had also been less than smooth and Sweden had topped our group in qualification. When you look at the players available, it is hard to understand why: Peter Shilton, Terry Butcher, Des Walker, Mark Wright, Stuart Pearce, Gary Stevens, David Platt, Glenn Hoddle, Chris Waddle, John Barnes, Bryan Robson, Paul Gascoigne, Peter Beardsley, Gary Lineker. There are some legendary names there. Hoddle was still playing well in Monaco but didn't even make the squad. The ability was there but it still hadn't quite clicked. As an example, England lost that game against Uruguay and went into the World Cup as long shots to win it.

The reality of that tournament is very different from how it is remembered too. In the group we drew our first two matches and it was only a 1-0 victory against Egypt that saw us move on to the knockout stages. We then needed extra time to see off both Belgium and Cameroon before losing against the Germans in the semi-final on penalties. It meant that in seven games we only managed to win one in normal time. But the results can never tell the story of that World Cup. Every game in the knockout stages was epic. The drama of David Platt's winner against Belgium. The rollercoaster against Cameroon that was eventually settled by two Gary Lineker penalties, his first a late equaliser to force extra time and the second to win the game. He must actually have had ice in his veins.

As a fan, it was a crazy time. There were parties in the street as the pubs emptied and, for a while, we really felt that it was our year. I was just 17 and it is still one of the most memorable times of my life. It felt like the whole country came together. I can remember watching all the games in a pub in Welling called The Station.

It was before big screens and everyone was crowded around this little screen on the wall. You could barely make out what was going on but the atmosphere was electric. I used to record the games at home and watch them again when I got in so I could see them properly.

One player captured everyone's imagination. Ask any football fan of that generation, who watched the 1990 World Cup, and they will most likely name Paul Gascoigne as the best English player they had ever seen. It wasn't just his undoubted ability, it was how he played. He had an arrogance and he stamped his personality on every game he played.

In England, we have a history of talented players who never quite produce their club form for their country; John Barnes, Glenn Hoddle, Steve McManaman, Frank Lampard, Steven Gerrard, Paul Scholes and Chris Waddle spring to mind. The argument is always that we don't use them properly or that they don't get as much of the ball as they do at club football. Gazza put an end to these excuses; every game in that tournament he went out and grabbed it by the scruff of the neck. He wasn't waiting around for someone to give him his chance, he was going to take it. He was named in the team of the tournament and looked genuinely world class.

We all laughed at his antics and marvelled at his football. When he cried after the booking that would deny him his place in the final, we felt his pain. We all remember Lineker mouthing 'have a word him' towards the England bench. What we might have forgotten is that Gazza put aside his anguish and seemed to play with even more determination after that booking. In the end it was all in vain, but we had found a new hero, who had the potential to compete with the very best in the world. I returned to training the next season knowing that Spurs were the team everyone was going to want to watch.

10

Is Gascoigne Going to Have a Crack?

MY SECOND pre-season was easier than my first. I remembered Paul Allen talking about the fact that when you do one, you keep a level of that fitness and it helps you in the others that follow. I still hated every bit of it but I coped much better second time around. I was now a second-year YTS and I had high expectations for myself. After the previous season's success, I was hoping for an equally successful or even better campaign. There were some excellent first-year players who would add to our team, including Jeff Minton, Kevin Watson, Darren Caskey and Nick Barmby. Caskey and Barmby had been at Lilleshall, so we hadn't seen much of them, but from minute one you could see that Barmby was a bit special. I was going to have to be on my toes to keep in front of him. We both played in a similar position and had a similar style of play.

I had reason to be hopeful, though, as during pre-season Ray Clemence took me aside and told me that I should be looking at playing for the reserves that season and not the youth team. This became my focus, until my next conversation with management. I then had an even greater boost when Terry Venables took me aside and told me to forget the reserves, I should be aiming to make the first team squad. It was just what I needed to hear and my performances in training and pre-season matches improved as a direct result of what had been said. I felt good in pre-season and I was performing well. Rather than looking over my shoulder at Barmby, I was trying to put pressure on Paul Moran and Phil Gray who were the two reserve team forwards. Both were excellent footballers who were destined to have good careers. But their time at Spurs had stalled and they were no longer being considered as potential first team players, but more as two players who could earn the club some good money in the transfer market.

This is probably a good point to now explain how the first team squad worked. Spurs had about 40 to 50 professional footballers with just two available teams for them to play for. This meant that every week there would be at least 15 players not even getting changed for a game. A few would go out on loan but you would still have lots of players training in the week with no action at the end of it. If a YTS player was looking promising, they would then get drafted into the reserve squad or occasionally even the first team ranks. The knock-on effect would be even more players sitting in the stand at the weekend.

Why did they keep so many players? Money! John Moncur stayed at Tottenham for eight years because he was too good to be let go for nothing. Every time he came to the end of a contract, they offered him a new one, knowing eventually they would get good money for him. But John was never really given a fair crack of the whip. Before the Bosman ruling you had no choice and if your club wanted you to sign another contract, as long as they matched your wages you had to sign it. When the Bosman ruling happened, you could leave at the end of your contract, but at this time that wasn't the case. You were only available for a free transfer if the club released you. But players didn't have to leave just because someone came in for them. Some just enjoyed the lifestyle of playing for Spurs. They were looked after, well paid and content. When they got into the last few months of their contract, they would go out on loan and make all the right noises about wanting to move on. These were very good players who were worth a lot of money in a transfer fee. On loan, they would do well and offers would come in. The club would then renew the contract due to not wanting to lose them for nothing. The player would then have a 'change of heart' and decide not to leave. Now, though, they were on another contract and so the cycle would begin again.

Being a success at Spurs was all about momentum. All the while you were on the rise, the club would keep pushing you.

You would play above your age and get in front of players that had fallen into the no-man's land, neither considered good enough to challenge for a first team place or bad enough to release. At the end of every season, a handful of these players would need to be sold to make space for the new intake from the second-year YTS boys. Bargains could be had if you knew your stuff. Sometimes these players would come back to haunt you. Football is full of stories of lads not getting a fair chance at one club then going off to another to rebuild their career. While I was a player the club believed had potential, it was important that I kept my momentum going, and I tried to ride it all the way to the first team.

As well as pre-season went, I had a bit of an alarm in one of the games. I got tripped up and, as I fell, I felt my left knee lock for a second. It was a little uncomfortable for the rest of the match, but I managed to play without any real problems and in training on the Monday I felt fine. I started the first game in the youth team and managed to score. I was then called up to the reserve side and came on as sub.

Ray Clemence was the manager of the reserve team and he was a legend in the game. He was 40 when he retired from playing, and even then that was only because of an achilles injury. He was still Spurs' first-choice keeper at the age of 39 and, with his enthusiasm for the game, who knows how long he would have gone on for. His love of football was infectious. As a manager, he had a great eye for detail and was incredibly professional. He is known as a gentleman and I can vouch for that. Ray was another person that I learned a huge amount from in a short amount of time. He had won the First Division six times and the European Cup three times. It is very difficult to do justice to the man in a few words; he was a one of a kind, and the world is a worse place without him.

My next appearance was back in the youth team, and although I didn't score, I had one of my better games. I started the next match for the reserves and scored in a win away to Reading. Again, I was very pleased with my performance and I could really feel the momentum building again. Back in training on the Monday I felt some discomfort in my knee, and had to drop out. I ended up missing the next game and so two weeks after the Reading win I was back in the youth team. I scored four goals in the next two matches and had no problems with my knee. Once again, I was called back into the reserve side. I was in the starting line-up again and was playing well. The ball went out wide and I made a run to the near post. The ball was slightly too high and I couldn't quite reach it. When I landed, I felt my whole knee go sideways and it collapsed under me. I went to stand up but my whole leg felt limp and I collapsed again. I was now getting worried. I wasn't in pain, I wasn't in anything; I couldn't really feel my leg. Alex, the reserves' physio, came on to treat me. He told me to tense my leg. I tried but I couldn't. He asked again, but I still couldn't do it. It was like it was someone else's leg; I could see it laying there, but I had no control over it. In the end they stretchered me off.

I reported for treatment on the Sunday to John Sheridan, the club physio. He pulled my leg about a bit and was pretty sure he knew what the problem was. He thought I had damaged my cruciate ligament, which is the main ligament that basically connects your thigh bone to your shin bone. There were two possible courses of action available back then. You could build up the muscles around it and try to play on or you had an operation. In the not-too-distant past it was a career-ender but recently more and more players were coming back from it. I now had a choice; the problem was I didn't yet have a professional contract. The operation would put me out for the season, and I couldn't do that. I felt like I actually had no choice and had to try and get through the season.

I ended up playing in less than half the games that season. If I started, I rarely got through the whole 90 minutes. I was in and out more times than the hokey-cokey. Occasionally, I would play two or three games on the spin and a couple of times I earned my way back into the reserve side. I was actually finding the youth team football easy and could get through matches having played well, even in pain from my knee. I just couldn't consistently get to the levels I knew I was capable of. Every time I thought I was getting going, it would strike gain. My knee would swell up and I would have trouble changing direction. Then I would rest it and it would all start again.

I still managed to score 15 goals in the 22 games I played that year, and I got another winner's medal for the South East Counties Division One team. But the whole season was a fight against my knee.

In March, I had a confusing phone call from an agent inviting me to a meeting. When I turned up, Ollie Morah, Greg Howell and Stuart Nethercott were already there. Basically, Ray Clemence worked for this management agency and had told them that the four of us were being offered professional contracts. The agent wanted to sign us before anyone else got a chance. We had therefore been told we were going to become professionals by a man we had never met before. A couple of days later, I had to act surprised when I was called into a meeting with Terry Venables and offered a two-year contract. I took the agent's number but I decided to do the negotiations myself. Not that there were many; I just wanted to sign my name on the line and get my knee sorted. I thought going into the meeting with an agent would be getting ahead of myself and send the wrong message. I signed then and there, ten minutes after walking into the office. I then went straight down to John Sheridan and told him I wanted the operation. A very frustrating season was finished by April.

My surgeon was John Browett, the very best that money could buy. I was sent to his office in Harley Street but had to wait to see him for the next time he was in the country, as he spent a lot of time jetting around the world. He sat me on the treatment table and jiggled around with my knee. Then he yanked it to the side, popping my knee out. I screamed in agony and he casually popped it back. He told me that it was definitely my cruciate, and that he would have to open me up and see how bad it was. I had an keyhole surgery that afternoon.

When I woke up, he came to see me and said, 'We had a look, Mr Potts. There was some damage to cartilage which we were able to mend. There was also damage to your anterior cruciate ligament. That damage was very severe. It looks like it is an old injury, probably when you were about 12. We will need to reconstruct your knee, but I feel it is only fair to tell you that you may never be able to play football again.'

With, that he walked out.

You know the feeling when you lose your phone, or keys or some money and it is a mixture of shock and dread? Where you feel physically sick for a second? It's almost an out-of-body moment as the realisation hits you that you have lost them. That was how I felt. But the emotion didn't go away. I'm not sure it ever did.

I was booked in for the operation for a few days before the FA Cup Final as again Mr Browett was going back out of the country. I rang the club to let them know what had happened and they told me to report to the ground for treatment. I explained that my knee was still sore and a little swollen, and that the only way in was by train and that I had no crutches. They still insisted I had to come in. I managed to get in without too many problems, but I was in quite a bit of discomfort. You can imagine how annoyed I was when I got there and John Sheridan told me there was nothing they could do or see so soon after the operation, and that I shouldn't have travelled in.

On the long journey home, I started to feel some pain and, when I went to look at it, I could barely get my tracksuit bottoms over my knee as it had swollen so much. By the time I got to London Bridge it was pushing against my tracksuit bottoms and felt red hot even through the material. When I got off the tube, I couldn't take a step. I had to ask someone if they could tell a guard I was down there. Eventually a guard turned up and I had to suffer the embarrassment of stripping to my boxers so I could show him my knee. He then called for help and I was lifted all the way up about four sets of stairs to an awaiting ambulance. The ambulance dropped me at Guy's Hospital, a short distance from the station. They had no available wheelchairs so the ambulance driver had to carry me to the waiting room. I waited to be seen for four hours, and then I was taken to a ward and stuck on a bed. There were no pillows or blankets, just a plastic mattress. I sat there for another hour in agony before I finally saw a doctor. I can remember that on the bed adjacent to me was an old lady who was in a lot of pain. One of the nurses said that she just needed a couple of pillows to support her back. The lady was told there were no pillows.

When the doctor finally arrived, I told him about my knee. He looked at it and noted how clean the incision for the keyhole surgery was. I explained that I had it done at Princess Grace Hospital on Harley Street. He immediately changed and refused to treat me, saying it was more than his job was worth, and he would be putting himself in a position where he could be sued. By now, my mum had turned up having been driven by one of my neighbours: David Wagner's football-hating dad Malcolm, funnily enough. They asked if an ambulance could take me to the Princess Grace Hospital as I was still unable to put any weight on my knee, but they were told no. They asked for a wheelchair to get me to the car, but they were told no. They asked for crutches to get me to the car, but they were told no. Not because the hospital was being difficult, but because there was nothing they could give me. In the end, my poor mum and Malcolm had to carry me down the hallway and to the car.

Guy's had at least phoned ahead to Princess Grace, and when we arrived there were two doctors and three nurses to meet me at the door. I was put on a fancy new wheelchair complete with leg support. I was then taken straight to my room, which was bigger than my living room. While we walked, the two doctors discussed my knee and, by the time I was lifted into my bed, the nurses had already been sent to get what was needed. A pot of tea and a tray of sandwiches were bought for my mum and Malcolm and the nurses explained to us all what they were going to do. I have always had a bit of a phobia towards needles; even now I have to look away if someone has an injection on the television. Of course, it was decided that they would syringe out the fluid. A nurse entered with the biggest needle I had ever seen. It was like a scene out of *Carry On Matron*. Four times they tried to drain the fluid; the last time they went through to the bone, which was like an electric shock. On the fifth go, my leg was shaking so much they couldn't get the needle in. Finally they gave up. I had to just stay at the hospital until the swelling went down naturally. As soon as the knee was back to close to normal, they were going to go ahead with the operation.

* * *

The 1990/91 season is a stand-out one for Spurs for many reasons. It started on a wave of euphoria after the previous summer's World Cup. Gary Lineker and Paul Gascoigne had been two of England's star players and every Spurs fan hoped they could bring their form back to the First Division. The problem was that the club had hit a bit of a financial blip, and there was even talk of possible administration. This meant that out of the threadbare squad from the previous year, only Justin Edinburgh was added, being brought in from Southend United. Initially he signed on loan and eventually joined for just £150,000 in January. Justin was a great addition, not only for his football ability but also for his personality. He looked like he just appreciated the opportunity he was given and was going to make the most of it. I never saw him without a smile on his face and he was as friendly to the youth team players as he was the first-teamers. It is a shocking that he was taken so young.

The season started well and after 17 games Spurs were in third place, and still in both cups. Gazza was playing out of his skin and the rest of the players started to become very reliant on him, but the problem was that Spurs had overplayed him. Gazza was still only 23 and had already played over 150 league games in his career. He was starting to have problems with his groins and when he was struggling or missing the results were suffering. By the time February had come around, the FA Cup had become the priority for Spurs and the rest of the season was all about making sure that Gazza was fit enough to play in the ties. He was almost single-handedly dragging the team through them and overall he scored 19 goals that season in just 37 appearances, while Gary Lineker also scored 19 but in seven games more. Lineker also took the penalties.

In the league, Spurs won just one of their last 20 matches and dropped down to tenth. At the same time they won six FA Cup ties. When you look at the footage of those games, it was all Gazza. On 14 April they played Arsenal in the semi-final. I am not ashamed to say that I was rooting for Spurs that day, and not just because I would be making a lot of money from my ticket allocation if we got through to the final. A couple of the first team players, who will remain nameless, had negotiated a great price for FA Cup Final tickets and were offering to buy as many of our allocation as we wanted to sell. The semi was on the day I was due to be released from hospital, so there was no way I was going to be able to go. I knew that if Spurs won I was going to make a couple of thousand pounds. I didn't know who it was buying the tickets and I didn't care. I also put £300 on an Arsenal win so that whatever happened I would be quids in. I wouldn't get away with that in the current climate but in those days players were always betting on football and could even place bets in the players' lounge. The money wasn't the only reason I was supporting Spurs that day. I loved their style of football, and these players were my friends, so it would have felt disloyal to support anyone else. I was now a Spurs fan!

Gazza ran the show, and his free kick was yet another example of the ability he had. He was also heavily involved in Spurs' second goal. The other players said he was like a maniac in the changing room before kick-off, like a man possessed. Lineker also stepped up that day and was always a man for the big occasion. Gazza's performance was even more remarkable in that he'd had a double hernia operation just a month before the game. In the end they had taken advantage of the gap between the quarter-final and semi-final and booked him in for the operation.

Between the semi-final and the final, Spurs brought in a financial advisor named Nat Solomon to help try and prevent the club from going into administration. Solomon strongly recommended selling Gazza to Lazio. This meant that going into the final Spurs had already accepted an £8.5m bid from the Italians. The club needed this money to keep the wolves from the door.

* * *

The Princess Grace Hospital was incredible. When I awoke from my operation my leg was attached to a machine that constantly bent and unbent it so that it wouldn't stiffen up. I was immensely grateful for this as I could still remember the pain that Mark Robson had gone through with his knee after having a similar operation. Robbo had been injured by a shocking challenge from Nigel Martyn during a reserve match. He had been a great young prospect, who was technically outstanding. Even after his horrific injury, he still had a couple of great seasons for West Ham. The problem he had was that after his injury he couldn't bend his leg for months. In the end it calcified and the only way he could bend it was by the physios physically cracking it every day. I used to have to leave the room. He was in agony as they cracked his knee, trying to bend it a little further each day. The noise as they forcible bent it was like popcorn cooking. Thanks to the machine, I would have none of those problems.

I wasn't allowed out of bed for the first 24 hours and I had a call button by my side. I could literally order anything and the nurses would get it for me. In the room was a television with hundreds of films I could watch. It was like staying in a posh hotel. The food was of Michelin star quality. The problem was that my tastes were more greasy spoon than fine dining, and there was nothing I could eat. When my sister used to visit, she would phone ahead and ask what was on the menu. I would then order what she wanted, and she would bring me a McDonald's. She used to love it.

In the end, one of the nurses cottoned on and spoke to me about it. I thought I was in trouble, but she just told me I could write down on the menu anything I wanted and they would get it in for me. I was eating KFC, McDonald's and steak most days. I was so grateful for the treatment I received; the nurses were brilliant. They couldn't do enough. They would sometimes come and sit in my room and watch TV or chat to see out their shift. They were run off their feet and knew they could get a bit of a break with me. The rest of the patients were used to private care and saw the nurses as 'the help'. I would sometimes hear them shouting at the nurses; they were so rude. The nurses knew that I was grateful for any help they could give me.

I left the hospital in the early hours of Saturday, 18 May 1991. I had already been told by John Browett that the operation had been a success. I had on a leg brace that ran from the very top of my thigh down to my ankle, and I couldn't walk without the aid of crutches. In the afternoon, I watched the FA Cup Final from the comfort of my bed. My mind was already set on my recovery and I wasn't going to have much of an off-season break, but I didn't care. I was keen to get my rehabilitation started. I was determined to come back stronger than ever and ahead of expectations.

The FA Cup Final was very much a tale of two stories. Number one was Brian Clough. He was nearing the end of his time at Nottingham Forest and there was a lot of support for him. Incredibly, despite winning numerous league titles and European Cups he had never won the FA Cup. Many saw this final as a fitting end to his time at Forest if he could finally win the one trophy that had eluded him. On the other hand, those who wanted Spurs to win were also rooting for Gazza. He had ridden the wave of hysteria from the World Cup and almost single-handedly got Spurs to Wembley. Everyone wanted a big performance from him. It had been a long time since England had a player who played with his style and freedom, and it felt like the final was another step on his journey to the very top of world football.

I watched the game on television laying in my bed, and you could see straight away that things weren't right. Before the game, when they zoomed in on Gazza's face, he looked manic and out of control. Again, in the weeks and months that followed, stories of his behaviour before the final started to appear. He was actually given Valium to calm him down at one point. Even before his tackle on Gary Charles he had made a couple of wild challenges, one of which – on Garry Parker – he could easily have been dismissed for. After Gazza had fouled Charles, I was completely focused on him. He was limping around and, when he was standing in the wall for the Stuart Pearce free kick that gave Forest the lead, you could clearly see the pain etched on his face. When he crumpled to the floor after the goal had been scored, the final lost a lot of its meaning to me. Although I still celebrated the victory, it felt slightly hollow after Gazza's injury. I just hoped it wasn't anything serious.

My favourite moment of the final was Paul Stewart scoring the equalising goal, as I had seen what a tough start to his Spurs career he had been through. That year was a turning point for him. He was converted to central midfield and even got a call-up for England. All the youth team players were a bit scared of Paul as he always looked in a bad mood, but he had a wicked sense of humour and could be quite funny. I could still remember that when I first joined the club, he was a target of the boo boys. Some of the stick he got was awful. He had been signed for a big fee at the same time as Gazza and he had not settled immediately. He was away from his family and he found it tough.

We used to get breakfast at a café next to White Hart Lane, and I can remember seeing Paul sitting alone one morning looking like he had the weight of the world on his shoulders. I felt so sorry for him. It seemed strange to feel sorry for someone who was living the very life you longed to live, but football can feel like a very lonely place when things aren't going well. Luckily he was a strong character, as he has shown in recent years that made public the awful abuse he suffered as a young boy playing for his local team. Terry Venables showed a lot of faith in Paul by sticking with him and, in the end, he proved the doubters wrong.

We went on to win the final thanks to Des Walker's own goal in extra time. It was surreal later that evening to see pictures of the team celebrating at Gazza's bedside complete with the FA Cup; it was the same bed I had slept in the night before.

11

I'm Doing Nothing
Until He Gets One

THE TURMOIL behind the scenes came to a head at the start of the 1991/92 season. Terry Venables put up £3m of his own money and managed to convince Alan Sugar, known today for his role in *The Apprentice*, to match it. By now Spurs were £11m in the red. The £8.5m fee for Gazza had dropped to £5.5m after his FA Cup Final injury, and they were in trouble. The Midland Bank, the listening bank as it called itself, wasn't listening, and it looked like the club might actually go into insolvency.

The money from Sugar and Venables managed to rescue Tottenham Hotspur and on paper the partnership seemed like the dream team. Venables had overall control over the football and Sugar was in charge of sorting out the finances. The only problem was that Peter Shreeves was brought in as team manager. I can only comment on what I saw that year, and, in my opinion, he was a terrible boss. Venables had been approachable and was liked by everyone, whereas Shreeves barely spoke to anyone. Training lost its intensity and the results suffered. In the season he was there, I don't think he even said good morning to me and I was not alone. The players complained that his training was poor too. Some players had even taken to doing extra sessions as they felt they weren't fit enough. It was not a happy camp.

Gazza and I both reported to training on the same day, a couple of weeks after the cup final. It was only injured players who were there at that point. John Sheridan told us both to jump on a treatment table so he could have a look at how our knees were coming along. When Gazza took off his tracksuit bottoms, he had a leg brace that just went over his knee and had a hinge which meant he could bend his leg. You could set the bend so that the knee didn't go past a certain point. Compared to mine, it was like something out of the future. When Gazza saw my monstrosity, which went from hip to ankle and had no bend at all, he flipped. He told John that until they got me the same knee brace as he had then he wasn't doing anything. In effect he went on strike. It was only once he knew for sure that one had been ordered that he let John check out his knee. This was my first real experience with Gazza, and was typical of the kind of man he was.

All the young players were obsessed with Gazza. We used to watch his every move and would always stop and watch him train whenever we had a chance. He was usually the topic of conversation and there were always stories about his latest antics. Despite being the best player, he was also one of the most approachable first team squad members. He would offer youth team players bits of advice and would often join in with our training when the first team finished early. If it wasn't for his issues, he would have made an excellent coach. From outside of the club, I would imagine that would surprise a lot of people. He was more complex than you would imagine and he was incredibly focused on his football. He was highly competitive and even in training he would push himself to his limits. He once told me that he had nearly been released by Newcastle on two different occasions. The second time, he had put himself on a fitness regime where he would go home from training and work until it was too dark to carry on. Jimmy 'Five Bellies' Gardner took the role of coach. This was a turning point for him and his debut came soon after that.

Through the whole of my rehabilitation, Gazza ensured that he was never given preferential treatment, and I will always be grateful for that. We are both very competitive and everything turned into a contest. In professional sports that is considered a good thing but in my regular life it is something I have had to work very hard to control. Even when they measured how far we could bend our legs, we would compete to see who could bend it further. The training ground was a horrible place to be at this time. We couldn't join in with the rest of the squad so always felt separate from everyone else. Injured players are quickly forgotten at a football club. If you can't contribute then you are almost made to feel embarrassed to be there. Even someone as talented and valuable as Gazza would feel like he was being sidelined. Gazza wasn't happy with Shreeves, and you could tell that he felt he had been pushed into the Lazio deal due to the financial problems at the time. Now he was being ignored, as if he had already left for Italy. If Gazza had any issues he would go above Shreeves and straight to Venables. I don't think he was alone; a lot of the other players seemed to do the same thing. I think John Sheridan picked up on Gazza's frustration, so we did a lot of our rehabilitation at a local health club.

John was absolutely brilliant throughout the whole process. There are two types of physiotherapist. One is what you would call a club physio, who is all about getting you back on to the pitch. You feel sore? Don't worry, get out there, it will be fine. These are the physios that managers like. An injured player is like a leper at a football club; coaching staff actually get annoyed at players who are injured. They want them out on the training pitch. This kind of physio can cause damage, though. Players can be rushed back too soon after unnecessary injections, and long-term consequences ignored. The second type is a player's physio. They see the players as being under their care and make sure that you are right mentally and physically. These physios regularly have to go to battle with coaches and managers over the players they are looking after. They don't always win but they try to do what is right for the player.

John was the second one. You really felt like he had your best interests at heart. Before joining Spurs, he had had great success at Luton Town, a small club at the time with little money. On realising the results that John got with injured players they actually implemented a strategy to get the most out of him. They started signing players, on the cheap, with a history of injures. These were often people who were considered too much of a risk because of their medical histories, such as Steve Foster and Ray Harford, who would go on to have great careers with Luton. John is someone who I am sure is remembered fondly by everyone who came under his care.

At Spurs there was a really nice little gym, well it was more like a private health club, but getting there used to be a traumatic experience. It was a two-minute drive from Mill Hill but you had to go across a double dual-carriageway. Gazza used to think it was funny to just accelerate across all four lanes, seemingly without looking. I disagreed. How he never killed us, I will never know. In the end, as soon as I knew John was ready for us to go across, I would sneak out and walk across rather than risk my life. Gazza's driving was something else. Sometimes he would go up to a roundabout and drive around it at a ridiculous speed about ten times. It was like a rollercoaster where you were actually fearful for your life. He would leave about a tyre's worth of rubber behind on the ground.

He did stuff that I found funny too. If he saw people with bags waiting for a cab, or hitchhikers, he would pull up as if he was going to give them a lift, but stop about 100 yards away. He would then wave at them out the window, seemingly signalling to them that he would take them with him. Every time they got near the car, he would move a little further away. It was a bit cruel, but hilarious nonetheless. Other times, if someone cut him up he would pull alongside them and point to their rear tyre as if it was flat. You would then see them in the rear-view mirror pulling over to check the perfectly inflated tyre as we drove off.

Gazza was like a kid playing with a toy car. He had this beautiful Mercedes and used to say to me 'close your eyes' while we were driving. Seconds later I would open them again and we were somewhere completely different, from a motorway to a village, or a high street to the countryside. Or he would say 'look at that car' and point in the distance, then again 'close your eyes'. Seconds later I would open them again and the car would be a distant dot in the rear-view mirror. I'm glad my eyes were closed because I dread to think how fast he must have been going, or some of the chances he was taking. His dad once told me that his biggest worry was that Gazza would die behind the wheel. I once asked Gazza about his driving after another near-death experience. It didn't calm my nerves to hear him tell me that he had a nightmare on his test. He said he should never have passed, but the driving instructor was a Newcastle fan so he passed him anyway. Gazza gave him a couple of free tickets to the next Newcastle game for his trouble.

The health club was great, and it just got us away from the pain of watching everyone enjoying themselves playing football while we couldn't. At first, we used to run in the swimming pool as the water would protect our knees. I am a terrible swimmer so Gazza used to make sure that John made us swim every day as he knew he would beat me. It would be so boring running in the pool wearing a buoyancy vest, but neither of us ever moaned. We were too busy trying to beat the other one. Also, we had both set ourselves the target of an early return to action. Mine was so that I could get a chunk of the season to try and impress as I only had a two-year contract. The danger was that half of it could pass without me kicking a ball. Gazza was desperate because his move to Lazio hinged on him getting fit, and the 1992 European Championship was at the end of the season; he was still hoping to play a part. For Spurs it was equally important he got fit as the Lazio money was key to keeping them above water.

After working in the pool, we would go up to the weights room. They had two step machines and we would try and outdo each other on them. Then we would go on every weights machine and try and lift more than each other or do more reps. Then it was sit-ups and press-ups, once again always trying to do more than each other. By the end of that stage of our rehabilitation I was as fit as I had ever been in my life. We used to do the step machine on its highest level and highest speed for an hour. On the weights, Gazza could lift more than me with his arms whereas I could beat him on my legs. We were lucky we didn't do ourselves another injury. John would get quite annoyed at us and tell us to take it easy. He was right. Often, the next day we would struggle to do half the things we should have done as we were pushing ourselves too far. We would often have to eat humble pie and admit that John was correct.

The first few months were hard. We both just wanted to be playing and would hate seeing or hearing about anything to do with football. We were just completely focused on our rehabilitation. To relieve the boredom, we started going out in the afternoons, after training. Gazza would send Jimmy to get a crate of Sol and a bag of limes and we would spend the rest of day drinking and playing snooker. Gazza would also get Jimmy to get £100 in pound coins. He would then play the fruit machine at the snooker hall, just aiming for the jackpot and never collecting until he got it. He would always leave having made money out of it. Money goes to money.

Other times, we would go to a luxurious private health club in the countryside that Gazza had been invited to use. There were always people wanting to give him stuff and he rarely had to pay for anything. Everyone wanting to get into his inner circle. Jimmy was always around, but they knew each other back before Gazza became Gazza, so Paul knew he could trust him. Some of the others I didn't really like. You could tell they just wanted a bit of the spotlight and I think Gazza knew as well. There was one hanger-on who was super-rich and ran a load of laundrettes all round London. He would do anything for Gazza. Gazza used to take advantage and send him off on errands all over the place. It was weird; it was like they both knew it was a false friendship but they both got something out of it anyway. We would finish training and Gazza would phone him up, and get him to do a load of jobs for him. Then later, he would get his moment and hang out with Gazza for a while – fame by proxy.

Gazza was very wary at this time of people. He would have private conversations with friends and family that would appear in newspapers. I would sometimes have conversations with him where he would narrow it down and it could only be one person. But that person would be a close friend or family member and it would drive him crazy, feeling like he was being betrayed. He was always very big on family, and loved being around people. He started to get very paranoid and his circle of friends was shortening. It has since come out that at the time he was being bugged by the newspapers, who had put a tap on his phone. It was a cruel thing to do and I am positive it affected his mental health.

As we became better friends, I started staying over at his house. We would go from playing snooker or being at the health club to going down his local pub and playing some pool and grabbing some food. At the time, Gazza shared a house with Paul Stewart, who would often go back and see family on days off. I would then stay over. Paul always looked like he had found a penny but lost a pound. One day, I woke up at Gazza's and started to get ready to go training, and Paul turned up. He gave me a cold stare and practically dragged me to his room. He had a right go at me for not making the bed. I genuinely thought he was going to hit me. Then he and Gazza cracked up laughing; it had all been a set-up. After that, I actually found him to be a nice bloke, and my opinion of him changed. I was still scared of him though. It was actually he who first gave me the idea for the book. He told me one day that I should be writing down all the things that me and Gazza had been up to as it would make a great story.

I was drinking quite a lot as this stage. We weren't getting wrecked, but most days we would have a few beers after training. If we had a day off we might have a bit of a longer session; that would be when I would stay over. What was weird is it was always based around competition, often playing pool or snooker until the score was something stupid like 54 to 55! We were burning so many calories every day that the drinking never affected our fitness, it just became a way of unwinding. I could certainly see how so many players end up with drinking or gambling problems. They were living away from home for the first time in their life. They were finished training by midday most days and most weeks got a day off during the week too. They had money in their pockets and low boredom thresholds. It was a recipe for disaster. I know for a fact that many of the players spent their afternoons going from bookmaker to pub and back again. If you had any kind of addictive personality it was not going to end well.

It was the case at Spurs that the management were very keen on the players getting married as early as possible. The thought was that if they were married then they would be kept busy and out of trouble. I'm sure they also thought it meant there would be someone to look after them as the majority, myself included, did not have a clue how to do the simplest of tasks. The club took care of every other aspect of your life. Had a toothache? The club would arrange a trip to the dentist and do all the paperwork. Passport running out? A new one would be sorted. They would even book your holiday if you asked. From the club's point of view they didn't want you worrying about everyday things, they just wanted you to concentrate on your football and nothing else. If they could get you to the game on the Saturday fit, relaxed and in the right mindset then they had done their job. The problems begin for many players when they leave the game and realise they do not have the skills to cope in everyday life.

We nearly got in trouble one time though. The millionaire who owned the health club in the country invited Gazza over to have a day on his farm, driving his collection of quad bikes. The man was a car freak; he had a genuine Formula One car in his garage and the truck for transporting it. It was an impressive thing to see up close. He clearly got off on having Gazza at his house and couldn't do enough for him. You could imagine him telling everyone at his club about his friend Gazza.

The quad bikes were brilliant. We borrowed some shotguns and drove around the farm like a couple of cowboys shooting various objects as we raced. Even writing it down, it sounds like a bad idea and sure enough it was. At one point we were racing and were heading through a gate, neither of us giving an inch. Anyway, long story short, Gazza went flying over the handlebars. We still had our knee braces on at the time and luckily the crash didn't do too much damage, but he had the first of his Lazio medicals coming up and it could have wrecked everything. These were the same bikes that nearly killed Ozzy Osborne a decade or so later. At the time, I was 18, nearly 19, while Gazza was 24, but I often felt like it was down to me to make the sensible choices.

With some of the stories he told me, maybe it was best that I did make some of those decisions. Gazza said that when he first started at Newcastle, he went to the bank to see his first wage packet. When he saw the amount on the screen, he went out on a shopping spree. After he had bought a new suit, some trainers and a shirt he went back to check his balance and it said that he still had £25 in there. Great he thought, and continued shopping. When he checked again it said £75. The bank must have made a mistake. Off he went shopping again. It was only when he saw one of the other Newcastle apprentices and told him what was happening with his bank account that the penny dropped.

'What colour was the writing, Gazza?' came the reasonable question from his friend in the youth team.

When Gazza checked he saw it was indeed red writing. He was £120 overdrawn on his first £29 wage packet. His dad had to take him to the club the next day and they arranged repayments for the money. He was now down to £24 a week for the foreseeable future.

Another time they were on tour in Spain, and the games were all on a huge field. Gazza was sitting with some of the other youth team players watching a match when a dodgy-looking Spanish bloke came up to them. He asked if they were interested in buying some grass. Gazza looked all around him before telling the bloke to do one. He then turned back to the rest of the youth team boys who had been listening to the conversation.

'Buy some grass? We're surrounded by the f***ing stuff, it's a bloody field! Does he think I'm stupid or something?'

He couldn't understand when the other players rolled about laughing.

Gazza was easily the most generous person I have ever met. I used to avoid talking about material things or commenting on his possessions as he would want to just give them to me. For example, I once said what a great car he had. It was beautiful – a black C-class Mercedes with tinted windows. He offered to give it to me. I explained that I hadn't passed my test, but he just said I could have it when I did. He once tried to take his watch off and give it to me when I said it was a cool watch. I had to walk away from him to stop him giving it to me. The first time I stayed at his house I said I wouldn't be able to because I had no change of clothes with me. In truth, I was actually a bit nervous because staying at Gazza's house when I was only 18 seemed like a big deal and I thought this was a good excuse not to do it. He just rang ahead and by the time we got to his house there was a pile of RIP clothes waiting. RIP was his clothes line that he had, but R.I.P. would have been more appropriate. They mainly made shellsuits and the designer was later arrested for crimes against fashion, I swear. If you get a moment, look it up on the internet. I thought I looked the business though and wore my RIP tracksuit everywhere for months. I still have it in a loft somewhere.

Gazza was also aware of his celebrity status and he would ring my friends and family to chat to them. It was all for my benefit; he knew the kudos it would bring. It was very difficult being friends with him. I was desperate to not be a hanger-on, just there to be a celebrity by association. But at the same time, it was great getting free stuff and living the celebrity life even if it was through him. There were moments where it all seemed so unreal, like playing pool in his local pub with him and Chris Waddle. I was actually laughing to myself at the ridiculousness of it. Two of the best players in the world and I'm having a few beers and playing winner stays on at pool! It was also difficult as I was very aware of people's reaction to me hanging around with Gazza. I didn't want to seem too big for my boots, or come across as someone who thought they were better than they were. I'm sure it is what a lot of people thought anyway.

I did have some great times though. I can remember spending the day with Gazza when he went on *Wogan*. It was amazing. We got our haircut opposite Harrods, then he bought a whole outfit from the shop for the show. He liked these suede Gucci shoes but couldn't decide on the colour so bought all the colours they had. Then, when we got to the BBC's Television Centre at White City, it was packed with people trying to get a glimpse of Gazza. It was crazy. The problem was that we were late so Gazza had to hide in the boot while Jimmy drove us in.

It was like that everywhere we went, which was why we tended to go the same places where we knew it was safe. People were unbelievable with how they spoke to Gazza. We would be walking down the road and they would lean out the window and tell him he was finished, or fat or worse. They didn't even do it in a mean way; it was like they felt that because of who he was they could do or say whatever they wanted. Despite this, I never saw him turn down a photo or an autograph. He actually went out of his way to chat to people and try and make their day.

I stayed with him while he got ready for *Wogan*, and then sat in the audience while they filmed the show. He even made sure he mentioned my name. Afterwards we had a few drinks in the green room and met Julian Lennon, John's son, and Alan Alda from *M*A*S*H*. Finally we ended up back at his local pub, drinking and playing pool. Gazza's brother-in-law was with us and he was thrilled to meet Julian as he was a huge Beatles fan. The day made me feel like a rock star and it was difficult not to get carried away as this was just a typical day.

Gazza's lifestyle had perks too. If he saw an attractive girl in a newspaper or magazine that he liked the look of, he would ring up the publication and leave his number. Nine times out of ten they would ring him back and he would go on a 'date'. He was never short of attention from the opposite sex. One of his 'friends' was actually married to a well-known page three girl. The phrase why go for a burger when you have steak at home was very fitting as he chased *anything* in a skirt. At the time, most men in the country would have happily switched places with him, but he still wasn't happy.

* * *

At the end of September 1991 we were four months into our rehabilitation and were ahead of schedule. Dave Butler took us out on the training pitch and we got to kick the ball about a bit. Gazza was unbelievable. Dave would throw the ball and we had to hit it on the volley or half-volley past the keeper. Every one he hit on the half-volley into almost exactly the same spot in the far corner. It was like a machine. He hadn't kicked a ball since the final in May but it was the best display of finishing I had ever seen. I wish I had a video of it; he was that good. After we were allowed to kick the ball, you could see Gazza had had enough. He wanted to be back playing. He was getting restless. This was not a good thing as his behaviour was getting more erratic. It was suggested that we could be given a few days off, so Gazza asked if he could take me up to Newcastle to meet his family and friends and get away from it all. He went above Peter Shreeves to Terry Venables. Venables was a bit unsure, but in the end said we could as long as we only went out to the Dunston Working Men's Club that Gazza's dad was a member of. We were buzzing. Venables, though, was right to be unsure.

There is always a lot of talk that Gazza would have turned out differently if he had joined Manchester United rather than Spurs. The feeling is that Alex Ferguson wouldn't have let him get up to his antics. I disagree. Firstly, I think Ferguson would have tried to change Gazza as a player. He was always about the team first, so I'm sure he would have stopped Gazza's showboating and curtailed his dribbling. I think Venables managed Gazza well, and the injury was something that could have happened to anyone. I can remember Paul Scholes and Roy Keane making some shocking tackles in their time. If you look back on Gazza's career before the injury, he had been player of the year in his second year, got on the World Cup team of the tournament in 1990 and carried Spurs in the year he got injured. Without the injury, he would have left for Lazio having had a very successful Spurs career. You also only have to look at Ferguson with Jaap Stam, David Beckham and Carlos Tevez. He would soon have lost patience with Gazza and moved him on. Gazza was a one-off and I am not sure what else Venables could have done. He was heavily involved in Gazza's life outside the club and was always checking up on him. In my time at Spurs, Gazza never missed a training session and worked as hard if not harder than anyone else at the club. Although he was drinking, it was no more than lots of players at the time, including many at Manchester United.

After training on the Friday, we got a cab to Kings Cross and we were on the train to Newcastle by about 1pm. We ordered some food and Gazza bought a bottle of champagne to celebrate. By the time we got to Newcastle we had finished two bottles of champagne. The journey was great and we spent the whole time talking about football. I was enthralled. I asked loads of questions but he was happy to answer them all. He gave me plenty of tips from his own game, and they were a revelation to me. He saw things so differently from other players, and it was fascinating to hear. For example, he said if you had a race to the ball with another player then have the battle for position straight away on your terms, before running to the ball. Most players would just try and get to the ball first and then have a tussle once they got there. It made perfect sense and is something I have always remembered. He had loads of these kinds of things that were unique to him. I feel we lost a talented coach when his demons overcame him. He even promised to show me some videos of him playing football as a kid when we got to his home in Newcastle.

By the time we got to Newcastle, it was early evening. We got a taxi straight to his parents' home. Gazza came from a poor background where they all lived in practically the one room, so as a result he is very close to them, and puts great importance on family. One of the main reasons he signed for Spurs was because they bought a house for his family. His dad was a really nice bloke. He was down to earth and clearly just wanted what was best for his son. It was quite touching to see how close they were.

We spent that night with Gazza at the working men's club with the rest of Gazza's family and friends. The club was like stepping back in time. There was still a men's lounge where the women weren't allowed, and in another room everyone was playing bridge. We spent the night playing snooker and listening to stories from Gazza's friends. It was great fun, but I should really mention some of those friends at this stage. There were a few people I met over the weekend who were lovely blokes to talk to but absolute wrong 'uns! One of them was a known drug dealer who had lost parts of his fingers through injecting bad drugs. Another had a reputation for using his fists, and some of the stories they shared made my hair stand on edge. You could tell they thought the world of Gazza, but it was clearly a good thing that he had moved away from Newcastle when he did.

Funnily enough, the only time I had ever heard Gazza mention anything untoward happening with him in Newcastle was when he got a bit cheeky with Billy Whitehurst in training and Whitehouse was threatening to kill him. These sorts of things happen all the time at football clubs, but Whitehurst had a reputation as one of the hardest men in Newcastle, and has often been considered to have been the hardest man in football. Gazza said he was genuinely worried for his life and had to ask some of his friends to smooth the waters.

As the night progressed, Gazza's mates were pleading with him to go out on the town, but he kept refusing. The end of the first night was a bit of a blur but I can remember going to a closed curry house that reopened and called back in its kitchen staff to prepare a meal and give a few more drinks to our group. The next thing I remember is the phone waking me up in a random hotel room that I have no recollection of. It was Gazza in reception coming to pick me up. I quickly changed and we went for some breakfast.

Newcastle United were at home, and we decided that we would go and watch. I could tell that Gazza was proud of his roots and he wanted to show off the club and fans to me. I thought London was bad, but in Newcastle Gazza was God. You could tell that the people identified with him and he was a real hero to them. When we got to the ground Gazza went to the main gates to get us some tickets. There was me, Gazza, Jimmy Five Bellies, Gazza's brother Carl and a few of Gazza's dodgy friends. At the time, Newcastle were struggling in the Second Division and St James' Park was half empty most weeks. The security guard on the door was a real jobsworth and turned Gazza away, much to the annoyance of many of the Newcastle fans walking past. Gazza could have gone above him as he knew so many people at the club, but he was annoyed. He argued that if he was going to buy a ticket, he would rather but a ticket for the Gallowgate End and stand among the real fans. So that was what we did.

It was certainly an experience. By the time we got in, the game had just kicked off. The ground was half full as we expected, but immediately behind the goal was where the hardcore Newcastle fans were, which meant it was still pretty packed at that end. We stood slightly to the side near the corner flag. It wasn't long before the fans noticed Gazza and started singing songs in his direction, ignoring the game. The match was poor so before long the whole crowd had moved and were packed in tightly around us. There was now a huge gap behind the goal with no fans. It was great fun and we were right in the middle of all the singing. I am sure that the players on the pitch were confused by the whole thing as from their view it would have looked like the whole home support had left. Eventually it started to get a bit out of hand, and we decided to head out of the ground. We went to a bar nearby and had a few drinks while watching the scores on the TV. Once again, the conversation turned to taking Gazza out on a proper night out in town. I wasn't keen and I don't think Gazza was really, but peer pressure started to kick in. You can imagine what it was like: 'We don't have to go out late,' 'We'll just have a few then back to the working men's club.'

In the end Gazza gave in. I tried by saying that I hadn't bought clothes for a proper night out. That problem was soon solved. A few hundred pounds later and Gazza had kitted me out for a night out in Newcastle, even down to my coat and shoes. Thankfully none of it was RIP gear. I now had no choice! We didn't even go home. I changed in the shop and Jimmy went and got some clothes for Gazza to change into. Without realising it, our night out had started a couple of hours previously. So much for just having a few. The night then was a tour of the pubs and bars of Newcastle. Gazza gave Jimmy a huge wad of money, and Jimmy bought everyone's drinks all night.

Jimmy was a strange one. He was clearly best mates with Gazza and they were like brothers, but there was a weird slant on their relationship. Firstly, I am pretty sure Jimmy was on a wage from Gazza, which meant he was obliged to do whatever he was told. Also, Gazza would abuse Jimmy something rotten. Jimmy seemed to love that, and seemed to be proud that he would let Gazza do what he wanted, like it was a way of showing how much he loved Gazza. Gazza would tell me stories where Jimmy would let him do things like hit him on his fingers with a hammer just to show his loyalty. It did, though, mean that at times Gazza pushed it too far, and Jimmy would disappear from the scene for a little while. I got the sense that Gazza needed some different friends, who wouldn't just let him do what he wanted and would stop him from doing things that were harmful to him and his career. I wanted to be that sort of friend, but at 18 I could barely make the best decisions for me. There were people like that around him, such as Chris Waddle, Glenn Roeder, Paul Stewart and Terry Venables, but he just wanted to enjoy himself and so would gravitate to the wrong types of people.

Anyway, as the night went on, the quality of the establishments went down. The only good thing was the fact we were always ushered straight into the VIP areas and never had to queue or pay to get in. The downside of this was we weren't very popular with the other clubbers. I started to feel a little uneasy and was on my guard. At one point we went in a club where the second floor was pitch black and full of people injecting drugs, just laying around the floor.

We made a sharp exit from that one.

Gazza's undesirables were really keen on us ending up at Walkers nightclub. Gazza really wasn't keen as it had a bad reputation, and he was actually pushing for us to go home. In one of the worst decisions possible, we finally relented and went. As predicted, it was dire. We hadn't been there long when I was led out the club by one of Gazza's friends. He explained that there had been an incident and that Gazza had been taken to hospital. He warned me that there was press everywhere, so he bundled me into a taxi and we set off for the hospital. Once there we snuck in and went to find Gazza.

Eventually we found him in one of the corridors. Gazza looked in pain, but was clearly relieved to see me. 'Pottsy, it's my knee it's f***ed. I saw the X-ray; they're saying it's nothing but I'm telling you it's f***ed.'

'What do you want to do?' I asked.

'We need to get back to London, get John to look at it. I'll get Jimmy to drive us.'

Gazza told me that he was on the way to the bathroom with Carl, when someone called his name. He said that he turned around and was punched in the face. Carl said that Gazza went down like a sack of potatoes; he thought he had been knocked out for a few seconds. Carl then tried to get the man who had punched his brother, but he disappeared into the crowd.

The problem was Jimmy had been drinking all day and his car keys were at his girlfriend's house. She wasn't going to be impressed with us turning up in the early hours. When we got to the house, she refused to let Jimmy in. There was a lot of screaming and shouting, and, in the end, he had to break a window so that he could get the keys. We then set off on the long journey to London.

We had been drinking for two days but every one of us felt as sober as a judge as the true enormity of what had occurred hit us. Gazza was in agony and I had to spend the whole journey holding his leg still as when the knee bent even slightly it would be excruciating for him. He was now seriously panicking. What if he couldn't play again? Would Lazio drop out the deal? Was this the end? He was sure that he was going to be crucified in the press, and he wasn't sure he could handle it. I told him that it wasn't his fault and that the truth would come out. The way I saw it, he would get some stick for being out, but, although he had been drinking all day, he wasn't falling about, noticeably intoxicated or acting in an inappropriate way. The mood of the whole night had been positive. He was just enjoying a night out in his home town. I now know I was being naive. One of the biggest questions from the whole thing was why the press were already waiting at Walkers before Gazza had even been assaulted, as they hadn't been anywhere else.

After what felt like a lifetime, we arrived back at the training ground. It was about 6am and John was the only one there. Gazza told me to go before any press got there, so I took the long train journey home, wondering just how much trouble I was in as well as hoping that Gazza's injury wasn't as bad as he thought.

Somehow, I never really got any fallout from the weekend. I think the consensus was that I had been the voice of reason for not wanting to go out on the town, although I'm sure that it didn't reflect on me in the best light. It was now a case of damage limitation. Gazza had a brand-new injury but luckily the reconstructed cruciate ligament was not damaged. It was a bad injury but one that he should make a full recovery from. The Lazio doctors flew in and they were satisfied that not too much had changed, although he was now going to be a few months behind schedule. Effectively, it meant that he now had no chance of making the England squad for the 1992 European

Championship in 1992. Without him, the team didn't win a single game and finished bottom of their group.

I went to visit him at the hospital after his latest operation, a few days after we had returned from Newcastle. When I walked into the room, his agent Mel Stein was there and he didn't look happy. There were also a couple of other people in suits, who didn't look happy either, so I almost turned around and walked back out. They asked if I was Anthony Potts and I told them I was.

'So you're the cause of all this trouble,' said one of them.

'Paul has just told us that it was your idea to go out clubbing in Newcastle on the Saturday,' said Stein.

I looked at Gazza for support but he gave me a look that said I was on my own. I tried to protest but Stein shouted me down. He told me that I was to be named in a lawsuit as a part of a litigation for damages. My heart was in my throat. I was sweating like a turkey at Christmas.

Then a smile appeared on Stein's face and everyone started laughing. Apparently I had gone white as a sheet, but all I know is my heart was beating like an anvil in a tumble dryer. Gazza was clearly not letting things get him down. I have never felt so relieved in my life! He had already got his brother by getting Paul Shane of *Hi-de-Hi!* fame to dress up as a doctor and pretend to trip and throw a urine sample all over him. It was actually Lucozade. Stein filled me in on what was happening and he sounded quite positive. There had been no reports of

Gazza doing anything untoward and he was clearly the victim. They felt that this was something that they could work with.

A few days later, it was announced in the news that Gazza had retracted his statement about getting assaulted. He was now saying that he couldn't remember what had happened. I was confused following everything I had been told and knew. The story I was given as to why he retracted his story was that the man who assaulted Gazza had only just got out of jail. He had been hired by one of the Newcastle papers to hit Gazza late in the night so that the newspaper would get the exclusive. The paper in question had links with organised crime in the city and Gazza's family had been threatened if he continued with his accusation of an assault. For this reason, Gazza had changed his story. This did not reflect well on him as it meant that everything he said about that night was put in doubt and the suspicion was that it was now his own stupid drunken behaviour that had led to the injury. Whether this is true or not I can't say for sure, but it certainly seemed to fit and explained a lot of the things that happened.

There was to be another fallout from the incident.

Glenn Roeder was going to be making the move to Lazio with Gazza. It had been thought that having him there would help to support Gazza and keep him on the straight and narrow. Unfortunately, this latest incident had meant that Glenn had decided to pull out of the deal. He felt that it was an unsafe environment for him to bring his family into. He felt all the furore constantly following Gazza was unhealthy and so he had decided to stay in England. Although Gazza was bitterly disappointed, he fully understood.

A week or so later, Gazza rang me. I could tell that it wasn't just an ordinary phone call and asked him what was wrong. He explained about Glenn and he said he had spoken to Lazio and they had agreed for me to go out there and take Glenn's place. I didn't know what to say. He told me that I would train with Lazio; Gazza had seen me play and he felt that it might even suit my style of football. I was gobsmacked and genuinely unsure what to do. On the one hand it was a fantastic opportunity that may never happen again, but on the other hand I still felt like I had a shot at Spurs. If I could get myself back fitter and stronger than I was before the injury then I felt like Spurs were still a good fit for me. I knew Terry Venables rated me; I had seen an interview where he had said he had high hopes for me. Also, it had only been a year since he had told me I should be aiming to be in the first team. In the end, the decision was taken out of my hands as Tottenham refused to let me go. I actually took this as a positive and used it to spur me on, as it made me feel like they still wanted me.

I didn't see as much of Gazza after Christmas as we were at different stages of recovery. My knee felt really strong and I was running and joining in, back in light training, but I had a new problem. Well, I say new, but once again it was really old problems coming back to haunt me. A very real danger when you get injured is that you can overcompensate and put undue pressure on other parts of your body. Often players coming back from long-term injuries begin to experience problems elsewhere on their body, and for me it was my ankles. I had always turned my ankles, but they very rarely prevented me from playing as I would recover quickly, often being able to carry on straight away. Now, though, I was starting to turn my ankles in the most innocuous situations. I would just be walking down the street and one would go. It was like having chocolate ankles, they were so weak. It was also incredibly painful when it happened, so I would feel physically sick and have to sit down until the feeling went away.

I didn't want to say anything to Spurs as I was desperate to just get back to training like normal, but I now couldn't train without having my ankles strapped up by the physios. Despite this, by the middle of January I was back training full time, several months ahead of schedule. I knew I had fallen down the pecking order, not helped by me trying to play on with my knee the season before. There were now five professional players in the first team squad who could play in my position. Paul Walsh had left but John Hendry and Gordon Durie had come in. Durie had caused quite a fuss, and it was the first sign of a rift between Terry Venables and Alan Sugar. Sugar had thought the club couldn't afford the Durie fee, but Venables had gone ahead and signed him anyway. It was also clear that Nick Barmby was being fast-tracked for the first team, and quite rightly. Venables loved him as he was exactly his sort of player. He was a very similar player to me and his rise just dropped me further down. In truth, I wasn't sure how I was even going to get a game. I was too old for the youth team, and there was only the reserves and first team that I could play for. Six into four doesn't go and I was the seventh, so for me to play it would mean there were four forwards not playing at all. Add to this that there were some excellent youth team players who would be getting signed at the end of the year, and it didn't look good for me.

With my ankles strapped I felt okay, and I was pleased with how I was training. It didn't go unnoticed, and Ray Clemence called me back into the reserve squad. He told me that I would be starting the next game, and he said I looked sharp in training. He was a good man and I could tell he was pleased for me. The fact he had put his faith in me, and was picking me in front of some excellent players, gave me a much-needed boost. I was so excited. I had managed to stay upbeat throughout my whole rehabilitation; I had been completely focused on getting back to where I was. Then on the Thursday before the game, I slipped in the mud and my ankle went under me. I knew it was a bad one. John Sheridan confirmed that I had damaged my ligaments, and he thought it could be as long as four weeks before I was back training. The news hit me like a sledgehammer. All the stresses of the last 18 months seemed to come crashing in on me. The journey home was long and painful but I didn't care, I hated my body. It had let me down again. My reaction was way over the top, four weeks was nothing in the big scheme of things, but it felt like the straw that broke the camel's back. Subconsciously I think I was becoming aware that I was broken.

When I got home, no one was in and I was glad. I couldn't face explaining that I was injured again. It had only been a couple of days since I had been saying that I felt good and had started to feel like I might get back to where I was before the injury to my knee. I went upstairs and lay down on my bed. I sobbed. I couldn't stop. I think I had managed to turn off all these emotions ever since John Browett had said I may never play again. I had just been focused on proving him wrong. It wasn't healthy. In the end it had to come out.

For the first time, I felt like just giving up and walking away from my dreams before they were taken from me. In football you see it a lot. The player who goes off the rails and then they never reach their potential. It is the chicken and the egg. Did they go off the rails when things started to go wrong, or before? The easy way is to go out on your terms, making it appear that you could have done it if you had really tried. It is the classic approach – better to fail looking like you don't care than try and still fail. Once again, my parents stepped in. They walked in on me sobbing like a baby. I could barely speak, and they were shocked. I had appeared so strong and focused throughout my injury. They put it out there – did I want to carry on? They would support me in whatever I wanted to do. For my whole life, becoming a professional footballer was all I had ever wanted. If I walked away now, I knew I would spend the rest of my life wondering 'what if?'

I had no choice.

I picked myself up, dusted myself off and went again.

The trouble was that my ankles were shot. It ended up being six weeks before I returned to training, and by the time I got myself back to match fitness it was the end of March. Once again, Ray was brilliant with me. He put me back into the side for six games and I put in some good performances. Then in the middle of April my ankle went again. I missed the last three matches, and I ended up finishing the season back where I started it; injured and in the treatment room.

12

Trial and Error

THE 1992/93 season saw the start of the Premier League and all the money that came with it. The league itself only came about because of the unfairness of the previous deal with ITV, in which the top five teams received 75 per cent of the money. It goes without saying that the other teams wanted a bigger share of the pie.

With the new deal, it was decided that the money would be split 50/25/25 – 50 per cent divided equally between the teams, 25 per cent based on where a team finished in the previous season, and 25 per cent based on how many times a team was on TV. For a long time, it looked like ITV were the only broadcaster in the running for the TV broadcast rights for the new competition as Greg Dyke, their chairman, was at the heart of the whole Premier League movement. It is widely thought that if Terry Venables had not been pulled from the negotiations because of a personal matter then it would have been ITV who won the contract and the history of football would have been much different.

Alan Sugar, whose Amstrad company had a deal to supply the majority of Sky receivers, stepped in for Venables at the meetings. He was not impressed with the deal on the table, realising the huge potential of football. It was due to be £262m over five years to basically show a game a week. It was reported that Sugar called Sky boss Sam Chisholm, telling him that he needed to make a bid. Sky offered £303m over five years for 60 live matches. Sugar did offer to not vote because of his relationship with Sky, but he was allowed to cast his after the other clubs, Arsenal and Manchester United aside, allowed it. The Sky bid won by one vote.

All of this also meant that I was one of the first playing members of the first Premier League.

Spurs were in the clear financially, and they were able to enter the transfer market again. Venables bought well, bringing in Neil Ruddock, Darren Anderton and Teddy Sheringham, finally filling key roles in the team. The Sheringham signing just dropped me one more place down the line of forwards. He was exactly the same sort of player as me, but polished and the finished article. He was so confident and he made everyone who played with him a better player with his appreciation of the game. Whenever I trained on the same side as him, I always played well, as he seemed to spot every run you made and always produced the right pass.

Our campaign started with a pre-season trip to Penzance in Cornwall to play in the Studio Ten tournament with Spurs, Manchester United, Liverpool and Plymouth Argyle. We all stayed in the same hotel and there were some top names there that weekend including Ryan Giggs, Robbie Fowler, Jamie Carragher and Jamie Redknapp. Liverpool in particular brought a squad worthy of most Premier League starting 11s and were managed by Phil Thompson. Off the pitch, it was carnage: fifty professional footballers in a hotel with a bar. On one night the players were allowed to have a few drinks. 'A few drinks' was code for in reality an incredible amount, and the bar got practically wrecked. There were fights, arm wrestling competitions and one of the hotel receptionists got to know several of the Liverpool players very well.

A few moments from that trip really stand out for me. Firstly, Ray Clemence had us all in for an early morning meeting on the day after the drinking. Just hours beforehand, Scott Houghton had ended up throwing and breaking a table. The meeting was hysterical because most the players in the room were still a little worse for wear as the drinking had gone on into the wee hours of the night. Scott in particular was still drunk and started giggling. This set off everyone else and we were all trying to stifle our laughs because Ray was clearly not very happy and we all had a lot of respect for him. It was like a group of naughty schoolkids sent to the headmaster's office trying not to laugh. The problem was that the angrier Clem got, the more Scott laughed. In the end the meeting got abandoned with everyone bursting into fits of laughter.

Another thing I remember is Glenn Hysén of Liverpool. He was injured so didn't play, but instead he would get a table and chair from the lounge and set himself up with a bottle of wine out on the driveway. He would be there when we left for the matches and he was still there when we returned about five hours later. On the night when it all kicked off, he was drinking 'Dirty Grandmas' at the hotel bar. These were basically pints of vodka and milk! The vodka was the bigger portion.

The football went well for me. In our first game we played Plymouth, and Paul Moran was up front. Paul was another one of those players who had the ability to see the humour in everything. His nickname at Spurs was 'Sparrow', as in cheeky Cockney sparrow. He was always joking and winding people up. Against Plymouth, he was giving plenty of verbals towards their centre-half, Andy Morrison. Now Morrison was no shrinking violet, and was a rival to Billy Whitehouse for the title of hardest man in football. In his book he talks about how he used to get in fights every weekend, and nearly died in one particularly violent bar brawl. Anyway, at the end of the game Sparrow made himself scarce before Morrison could get to him. But Morrison was persistent. He found out what hotel we were all staying in and tracked down Sparrow. Morrison gave him a dig, but luckily for Sparrow he held back or he wouldn't have been quite so chirpy.

We actually won the tournament, beating Liverpool 5-1 in the final. Jamie Redknapp scored the Liverpool goal while I managed to get on the scoresheet too. It was a wonder goal from out on the touchline near the halfway line and I hoped it was a sign of things to come. Mine wasn't even the best goal of the game, however. That was scored by Jeff Minton, a wonderful curling effort following a great dribble. Jeff was actually named player of the tournament above all the talent that was on show. It was Sammy Lee who picked him, so it was quite an honour.

Jeff was a year younger than me and possessed incredible ability. He was also deceptively strong, as shown when he won the arm wrestling competition after an epic battle that left one table broken in half. Jeff is an excellent example of how, in football, what you are allowed to get away with is in direct correlation to how good you are. Clubs will bend over backwards to accommodate the star players who miss training or are living questionable lifestyles away from the game but will quickly cut loose someone on the decline for the smallest discrepancy. Morally it is wrong and it often doesn't actually help the star, who feels like they are above the rules or drift into addiction. The problem is that often these issues occur later in life for the player and by 'handling' him the club can get success in the short term. Jeff was never that bad, but he certainly got away with a few things.

As a player Jeff was very well thought of at Spurs. I can remember first team players watching Jeff take free kicks and asking him to show them how he did it. Jeff was a contradiction though. He clearly loved his football and was like an encyclopaedia when it came to facts about the game, but he would sometimes skip training and go missing. He was so highly rated, though, that the only outcome would be that he would be called into a meeting with Terry Venables and then be given a pay rise to try and demonstrate how Spurs valued him. I can remember Paul Mahorn, a good friend of Jeff and a great person to have around a dressing room, saying that if it was him doing what Jeff was doing then he would have been out the door. In the end, Jeff played several games for the first team and had an excellent career in the lower leagues, although his talent possibly deserved more.

Unfortunately, the good start I made in Cornwall was not a reflection of the year I was going to have. You might find it hard to believe following some of my previous seasons, but the 1992/93 season was to be my worst season ever.

It started with most of my friends at the club leaving. Paul Gascoigne went to Lazio, Ollie Morah left for Swindon, Neil Smith signed for Gillingham, and Kevin Smith just left. Of the other players at the club I had grown up with, they had all either left, were in the first team or on loan. I genuinely felt alone.

This was also a bad year for the ex-Villacourt contingent. Steve Roast, Jason Peters and Dean Owen were all released by Southampton as was Danny Wareham from Charlton. Southampton also released their right-back that year. Kevin

Phillips was his name. He went on to non-league football where he changed positions to a centre-forward. He then couldn't stop scoring goals and rose through the leagues before signing for Sunderland, and over his career he scored nearly 200 league goals, almost half of them in the Premier League. He remains the only Englishman to win the European Golden Boot, having scored 30 goals for Sunderland in the 1999/2000 season. His release was yet another example of clubs getting it wrong. When I hear stories like that of Kevin Phillips it always makes me wonder how many potential stars were lost through poor talent identification.

Darren Hancock and Kevin Horlock were both also released by West Ham about this time. It was a shock as I honestly thought they were a certainty to make it as professionals. For Darren, this was his first rejection in football and I am not sure he ever felt quite the same about the game afterwards. It hit him hard and he found out his true friends. They were both disappointed with their treatment by West Ham, but that didn't surprise me as much! It was genuinely one of my favourite footballing moments when West Ham had to pay £405,000 to bring Kevin back to the club in 2003. I love these comeback stories; people like Jamie Vardy, Peter Beardsley and David Platt being released and then coming back to prove people wrong.

At the start of 1992/93, Terry Venables moved further behind the scenes and you no longer saw him on a day-to-day basis. Doug Livermore and Ray Clemence took over the first team management and Venables clearly didn't want to be a distraction. It was a popular decision to replace Peter Shreeves as the players never really got on board with him, while Doug and Clem were very popular. Doug was a proper footballing man and was hugely respected at the club. He was a huge Liverpool fan and paid me my greatest footballing compliment when he told Harry Redknapp that I was the closest he had seen to Kenny Dalglish. My eight-year-old self would have had a knowing look on his face.

Shreeves had done an excellent job in his first spell at the club, but it never really happened for him this time around. I guess having Venables still around couldn't have helped. The respect for Venables among the players was huge and it was always going to be tough taking over from him.

The impression was that Doug and Ray were reluctant managers, and that their appointment was more about steadying the ship than anything else. The rest of pre-season did not go well, and I spent more time in the treatment room than I did on the training ground. Then with the season approaching I was told that I was to be given a free transfer once it came to an end. I can't remember who told me or how I was told as I seem to have blanked out a lot of that season. It wasn't a shock; even I had begun to doubt that my ankles could sustain a professional career in football. With the benefit of hindsight, I should have gone to John Sheridan and told him about my concerns. Tottenham had world-class healthcare and I am sure that an operation would have given me a chance to rebuild my career after I had left. In the end it was my ankles and not my knee that proved to have the biggest impact on my future, never allowing me to physically get back to the required level.

I did make poor choices, but I wasn't helped by anyone that year. I was a young man in desperate need of some advice from people who knew football. Instead I had become the invisible man. It felt like days turned into weeks and into months, and everything I had worked so hard for seemed to be dripping away. I find it hard to believe that no one saw this. I know I should have been more forward and chased people up, forcing them to deal with me, but at the same time that wasn't my personality. I was desperately in need of some help but none was forthcoming. In the end, I was torn about what to do about my ankles as I was aware this was my last year and I had only played six matches in the last year and a half. I didn't feel like I could be out for any length of time. I needed to play games and put myself in the shop window.

A couple of months into the season, I potentially had a way out. Charlton contacted Spurs as they had heard I was available on a free transfer, and they wanted to take over my contract. Amazingly, Spurs made a U-turn and said they wanted money for me. It wasn't much, but Charlton were the team taking all the risks so they dropped out. I think that Spurs wanted to see out the year just in case I made a miraculous comeback. I loved Spurs, but I felt like they had hung me out to dry on this occasion. On reflection, I think they were still wary of me coming back and making them look bad.

I noticed a change in their attitude towards me. I would go into training, train and then go home. I had almost no interaction at all. I knew why; they were pushing other players and I wasn't part of their plans but no one gave me a second's thought. My agent had also disappeared and wasn't returning my calls. This was very strange as he promised the world when I signed with him! The season was just ticking away and I was in danger of leaving Spurs without another club to go to. Every day I came into training, put my head down and tried to work hard and impress the coaches. It didn't work. I got through to Christmas without playing a single minute of football and could not have been more on the outside of things. Time just seemed to be ticking away.

In October, Gazza came back for a game in the League Cup. It was good to see him, and he had loads of funny stories to tell. He was actually finding Lazio tough. Training was a lot more fitness-based, and he moaned about the warm-up taking about an hour. He just wanted to enjoy his football but found it very tactical and defensive. Gazza complained that they controlled every minute of his day, and you could tell he was lonely. He joined in training with us; it was the first time he had been part of a normal session at Spurs since the FA Cup Final. He was the best player by a country mile; no one could get near him. His appearance was all anyone spoke about for a week.

After Christmas, I decided to take matters into my own hands, but I didn't even do that properly. My ankles had been okay for a while and I knew that Spurs had done nothing to help find me a new club, so I decided to write to clubs and ask for a trial. For me, this was the least confrontational way of doing things. I should have got someone at Spurs to do it for me as they had more experience with this sort of thing. In a poorly thought-through decision I ended up writing to two clubs, Millwall and Charlton, as I wasn't sure that I would even get a reply. Happily I did; unfortunately they both offered me a month's trial. I didn't have a clue what to do. I didn't want to turn either of them down as I didn't want to burn my bridges so, in a decision as bad as Jason Cundy's cowboy boots, I decided to do both. This meant that Charlton had to wait for me to finish my Millwall trial, so they must have thought they were second choice. It also meant that Millwall couldn't extend my time with them if they wanted to and they thought I wasn't fully committed to them.

Good job, Pottsy.

Millwall were managed by Mick McCarthy at the time, and I have to say I was very impressed. I knew a couple of the players, Brian Lee and Andy Roberts, as we grew up in the same area, and went to neighbouring schools so saw each other at different footballing events growing up. In situations like this you have a kind of mutual respect even if you don't really talk. Andy was in the first team and doing

196

really well. You could tell in training that Mick was clearly a big fan of him and I was pleased for him as he is a very down-to-earth, modest man. Andy was a good player and was deceptively strong.

I felt at home at Millwall and was really enjoying my football. They had a small squad so the reserve group was basically seven or eight players who were either on their way up or on their way out. One of them was Ian Bogie, who was clearly very talented and had actually been touted as the next Paul Gascoigne when coming through the ranks at Newcastle. He was a very good player with a very bad haircut, which made some of my bad decisions look good. We also had Mark Kennedy training with us. He was a young player who was very highly rated at Millwall. He made his debut later that season while still just 16, and ended up taking the Jamie Redknapp route in signing for Liverpool before his 20th birthday. He looked destined for great things but his career seemed to fizzle out for some reason.

During my trial, Mark was certainly a player who was getting a big push. Brian Lee, meanwhile, was in a similar situation as me in that he was fighting to say at the club. I was pleased that he was there as he helped me settle in quickly. Brian is one of the good guys and got on with everyone at Millwall. During my time there, I just had one problem: Spurs refused permission for me to play in the reserve side. I was told that if I did so then I wouldn't be able to play for Spurs' reserves on my return. I thought it was ironic as I hadn't played for the reserves all season! The negotiations went backwards and forwards for a long time and, in the end, I had to leave Millwall without playing a game.

It didn't take a genius to know that there was no way Millwall were going to sign me. I was disappointed because I loved my time there and they had wanted me to stay longer. But without a deal on the table, I felt like I couldn't upset Charlton. Another great decision from me; you might see a pattern developing.

Charlton were another well-run club and I knew quite a lot of their players as they were my local team. I even knew the groundsman from nights out at The Station, but I got the impression that they felt I had rejected them already by going to Millwall first. Again, I felt like I did quite well in training but without playing games I knew it was pointless. I had another problem too. In my head I had pictured going on loan, getting a run of games and working my way back to form. In reality I hadn't played a match for more than six months, so it would be a big ask to hit the floor running. I started to doubt that, even if I got a chance to play, I would be able to really show myself to the best of my ability. The dispute with Spurs continued but in the end they said I could play for Charlton's reserves, but by then I was already at the end of my month's trial so I just had the one game to impress – against Arsenal at Highbury. It was two days before the end of my trial.

It was to prove to be a nightmare. I played up against Andy Linighan, who Arsenal had paid over £1m for. It was one-way traffic; I barely got a kick and, when I did, I felt rusty. I wasn't playing well but near the end of the first half I had a couple of nice touches and I felt like I was growing into the game.

At half-time they substituted me. I was devastated; my first appearance in more than six months and I didn't even make it to the second half. At the end of the game, I went to see the manager Keith Peacock. In another coincidence he was the dad of Gavin, who had gone to Bexley Grammar. Keith was very honest. He said they had other forwards at the club who were very similar in ability to me, and mentioned Kim Grant, who was the same age as me. He said they had invested a lot of time into Kim and knew him as a player inside out. Keith told me that they knew I still had some injury problems and they did not have the room in the budget to take a gamble on me. I couldn't argue with him, and he wished me good luck. I returned to Spurs in the middle of April and managed to make one appearance before I left. In the end it turned out that the reserve team rule wasn't even a real thing.

There was one moment that summed up that last season for me. There were a few of us doing finishing practice with Keith Waldron. None of us were playing at the weekend and enthusiasm levels were low. There were only a few weeks until the end of the season and I was still without a club to move to. No one at Spurs had spoken to me about it and my future was clearly being left to me. I didn't have a clue what to do. I had tried setting things up by myself with Millwall and Charlton, but that had clearly crashed and burned. I was incredibly frustrated. It was my turn in the shooting session and I tried something extravagant instead of just putting the ball in the goal. Keith, quite rightly had a go at me. I bit back, 'What's the point, it doesn't matter what I do, no one cares any more anyway,' or something along those lines.

Keith snapped back and told me that I'd turned down Millwall so what was the point in helping me.

The lack of communication was astounding, both from me and the club. We were on completely different wavelengths. It wasn't Keith's fault as he was only repeating what someone had told him. I couldn't stop thinking about that moment for weeks after. It's funny, but in low times you always look for someone to blame. It was tough, realising that I was my own worst enemy.

By the end of the season, following a very inconsistent year for Spurs, Terry Venables was back taking a more hands-on approach and started taking the training for the first team. He was still a great coach and results did improve, but as things turned out I wasn't the biggest name to leave at the end of that season. Alan Sugar actually sacked Terry Venables. He was fired for financial irregularities, before getting an injunction and being reinstated, only to be fired again and ordered to pay costs. Venables departed a couple of days before me. I'm not sure how much of his original £3m he left with, but his reputation was in tatters.

A year later it was announced that the club was now worth £100m. Alan Sugar is no one's mug.

Later, Venables became England manager and almost ended the country's wait for a major trophy at Euro '96 when football nearly came home.

My final day as a Spur was surreal. I felt numb all day. I turned up, trained, and then left for the last time. I didn't make a big deal of it, but I knew the significance. I had grown to love the club, but I had played eight games in just over two years. I think most of the players didn't even know it was my last day. In the end, it was to be my last day as a professional footballer; no one even said goodbye.

13

Lost

DURING PRE-SEASON ahead of 1993/94, I got a boost when Stoke City rang me and invited me to a trial game. I was determined to make the most of the opportunity and couldn't wait for the game to get started but, in the end, I should have known better. There were only three players who were there by invitation; everyone else just turned up on the day hoping for a chance. It was like *The X Factor* but for football. It was so bad that it was actually funny. Me and the other two trialists stuck out like sore thumbs as we were the only people there who could actually kick the ball properly. The three of us spent the whole day laughing as we watched the carnage around us. Stoke put us into about six different teams and rotated the teams every 15 minutes or so. The *X Factor* footballers were delusional; they really thought they were something. You could imagine them watching football on television and telling everyone that they could do better. Well, this was their chance and the results were comical. It was like when kids first learn to play football and they all just chase after the ball.

To be fair to Stoke, they did pull me aside and apologise at the end of the day, saying that it had been an experiment that went wrong. They asked me if I wanted to return for another trial but I thought better of it, and ultimately I went straight from Spurs to Dagenham and Redbridge. They had seen my name on the free transfer list and got in touch offering me a trial. On my list of poor decisions, this is definitely in the top five, which is pretty impressive given how long the list was by this point. Even Ian Bogie's hairdresser got more things right than me.

Dagenham and Redbridge were at this time the richest team in non-league football and were paying the best wages. They had a business model based on two non-league teams amalgamating and pooling all the resources and money. They sold one of the old stadiums, released half the players and carried on in a much stronger position. They had done this twice already. It sounds ruthless, but needs must and they had been very successful through it. They had eight non-league England internationals and were favourites for promotion into the Football League under manager John Still, who was already by then a legend in non-league football and it was immediately clear why. He ran the club in a very professional manner and the whole setup was very well organised. The reason it was a bad decision was the fact that Dagenham were part-time and only trained two evenings a week. This meant that the fitness I had built up through training full-time for four years started to seep away. On reflection, I should have tried to get a trial somewhere in league football. I did have a couple of teams that were interested but with Dagenham I didn't have to leave home. A poor reason for making a bad decision.

Pre-season could not have gone better for me right up to the point it went bad. In our first pre-season game we faced Spurs at Mill Hill. We won 1-0 and I scored the only goal, bent into the top corner from outside the area. It was my first and last angry celebration. At the end of the game Pat Holland came up to me and asked if the goal was a big f*** you to Spurs for releasing me. It was the first time he had spoken to me for nearly two years.

His name brings up mixed emotions for me. I have a lot of respect for him as at the start he was incredibly supportive and gave me great advice. His coaching and knowledge is second to none and I know I became a better player because of him. On the other hand, he was old school. In today's game, if he acted like he did then, he wouldn't last five minutes. Parents would be complaining and players would be walking away from the clubs he coached at. One of his main coaching techniques was to belittle you and make you feel awkward. At the end of training, we would play a small-sided game and he would join in. Some of us used to wait before picking up a bib until we saw what team he was on. If you were on his team it was a nightmare. Any mistake and he would shout 'AAAAAH' and throw his arms up in the air. He would call you names and shout in your face.

I felt fortunate to never really be on the end of one of his worst insults but many weren't so lucky. 'If you make it as a player, I will show my arse in Harrods shop window' and 'You're like a tart out there, you can come and work at my wine bar as a waitress' are two that I can remember off the top of my head. I used to laugh, but as an adult I know that he was responsible for destroying some players. It wasn't really his fault though; he was the product of his upbringing. In his time it was even worse. The idea behind it, of trying to separate the mentally strong from the weak, was solid enough. I'm not sure mental health was even considered a thing back then; if it had been then he might have been aware of the damage he was doing. I also know from stories I have been told by friends that he was far from the worst at this time.

I know at some clubs there were coaches who actually abused the young players. My friends at Villacourt were fortunate, during their time at Southampton, to not be one of the unlucky 45 youth team players to have been abused by their coach at the time, Bob Higgins, a vile individual who preyed on the young players' desperation to succeed. It wasn't like we hadn't all heard the rumours. There were always stories about the Higgins within football, but you just always thought they weren't real. The fact nothing ever got done made you think they were just malicious rumours.

I would bet that for every one who came forward when the scale of abuse in football was revealed in the 2010s, there are at least another 100 who have stayed quiet. I can only admire those individuals who have opened themselves up to the world. By publicly shaming their abusers they have hopefully set a precedent for others to follow and prevented further abuse taking place. Through coming forward and putting this in the public forum, they have held a mirror up to the conduct of football clubs and the associations that guide them and found them wanting. The braveness of these individuals, Paul Stewart being one of them, has to be admired and the progress and change must come so as not to waste this courage. Any child who has suffered abuse from the very people who are supposed to guide them and set them an example must know that they will be heard and that justice will be done.

I played six games in pre-season for Dagenham and Redbridge and scored in every one. I was playing well and I was already accepted as one of the lads in the changing room. They had a veteran centre-half called Tony Pamphlett, who I had watched as a kid when he played for Dartford. He had done the lot in non-league football and like John Still was a legend in the semi-pro game. He took me under his wing and really helped me to settle in. Tony loved a story, and the bar always used to be packed after training as everyone gathered around and got him to tell a few tales. The things he had got up to were outrageous, far worse than anything I had heard of in the professional game. He had no shame and would tell all the gory details. My sides used to ache by the time I got in the car for the journey home. He drove me to and from training and again would tell me stories about the teams I had watched as a kid with my dad. I would then go home and tell them to my dad!

Then at the end of the sixth match, I felt a lump in my hamstring. The physio treated it like he would have done any hamstring injury and it went away. In the meantime, Billericay came in asking if they could take me on loan. John Still spoke to me and he said he thought it was a good idea to build up my fitness and get used to non-league football. It made sense so I said yes. It was a good move. I liked the club, it was well run and the manager, John Kendall, had bought me with a specific job in mind. He wanted someone to play just off their main striker and knit the attack together. He had clearly done his homework and I could tell he had watched me closely. From minute one, I was completely at home.

Once again, my mum stepped in to support me. I still wasn't driving and there was no one from my side of the River Thames who played for them. She used to drive me to training and sit in the bar reading until training was over, then take me home again. She knew that it was the last chance saloon for me and couldn't do enough to help. My mum and dad would then take me to the games and watch me play. Then, after about four matches, all victories, the lump in my hamstring returned. The physio told me to rest it and gave me an ultrasound scan. In my first appearance back I scored, but by the end of the game the lump had reappeared. It was now about the size and shape of a golf ball. About two months this went on for; I would play, the lump would reappear, I would rest for a couple of weeks, it would go away, I would play, the lump would reappear. It was driving me crazy.

To keep my fitness I had been doing gruelling runs up and down the hills in the woods near my house. I was desperate not to lose the fitness I had built up over the previous seasons at Spurs. It was all the more frustrating for the fact that I was showing some glimpses of my previous form. For example, we played the league leaders Bishop's Stortford away in a cup tie. They ended up comfortably winning the league, but we managed to beat them 2-0 and knock them out. I produced my best appearance in what seemed like forever. I even scored a goal from in my own half, catching out the keeper who had advanced to the edge of his box. Even then, at the end of the game I could feel the lump in my hamstring starting to reappear. It was so disheartening. Knowing the past couple of seasons I had had, I'm sure you can imagine my state of mind. I was all over the place.

The physio at Billericay wasn't a qualified physio, few were in non-league, so the club paid for me to visit someone who was. I walked in the door, and without even giving me a check-up he told me that my back was out. It turned out that I had a problem with my sciatic nerve, which runs down your back and into your hamstring. He cracked my back into place and told me that the only treatment was rest. He explained that what had been happening was my resting would start to cure my back, and it would start to mend itself. Then the runs up the hills would put it back out. In trying to keep my fitness levels up I kept on just putting myself back to square one. The only cure was to rest it for a few months and have regular sessions with the physio. This meant that by the time I was back playing it would be March. I was gutted. I knew that complete rest meant my fitness would be gone by the time I returned. We were second in the league and pushing for promotion – three teams went up that year – and we were also doing well in the cups. It felt like my season was over, but I had no choice as I couldn't carry on like I was.

I then got a phone call out of the blue from Ted Buxton at Spurs. Ted was the chief scout and would go on to do the same job for England under Terry Venables. He told me that a club in New Zealand, Wellington United, were looking for a forward and a central midfielder. He said that Greg Howell was going and he asked if I would be interested. Coincidentally, I had been making enquiries to play abroad. Steve Roast, my old team-mate from Villacourt, had gone to Sweden to play and was loving it. The move sounded like it might be just what I needed. I told Ted to say yes, and the wheels were put into motion. There was a huge part of me that just wanted to get away from everything. In my head that was how I saw this, a chance to just put it all behind me. I was literally running away from my problems.

The only thing was I hadn't run or kicked a ball for nearly three months and my back still wasn't at 100 per cent.

I decided to blag it.

I told Wellington United that I was fully fit and boarded a plane for the 28-hour flight to New Zealand. That's never going to be recommended treatment for a bad back. I had to change at Auckland and can remember waiting at the concourse for my bags. They never turned up, so I was panicking. It was a big step to spend a year in New Zealand. I didn't even know where I was going to live. I hadn't slept and had barely eaten for 28 hours; my poor diet meant that the plane food was inedible except for two rolls about the size of a ping pong ball. Close to breaking down, and regretting my decision to leave England, I told an airport employee that I had lost my bags. He looked at my ticket and told me that my bags had been transferred to the next plane automatically. I then had to take my first run in three months to get to the boarding gate before my connecting flight took off.

New Zealand is a beautiful and unspoilt country. My flight from Auckland was in a biplane that flew low over the ground, and I got to see the amazing landscape. I could even make out the hot springs; I was almost disappointed when it was time to land. I landed in Wellington on a Saturday morning and was picked up at the airport. Greg had already been there for a few days. They took me from the airport to where I was going to be staying, with one of the club officials, Stuart Prossor.

They asked me how I was feeling. I told them my back ached, trying to sow the seeds in case I really wasn't fully recovered. They told me there was a game that afternoon and asked if I could play! In the end, I negotiated down to a substitute's appearance. It wasn't the best way to start my time in New Zealand. I came on for 20 minutes; I ached all over from the flight and my back felt like it was in knots. I barely got a kick and they must have wondered whether they had got the right Potts. Maybe they thought I was Steve Potts.

I loved my time in New Zealand. Everything about it was brilliant, except the football. The level was about the equivalent of League Two or maybe the National League. I just wasn't ready for it. I had lost my fitness, my ankles were playing up, and I was constantly worried that I was going to put my back out. Greg, on the other hand, flourished. He had put his knee problems behind him and played some great stuff out there. I actually thought that he might come back and go on to rebuild his career in England, but for whatever reason it never happened.

The life was great. Me and Greg had such a laugh. It was our first time away from home, and we took full advantage. It is a genuine regret that I wasn't fit when I was out there because if the football had also gone well it would have been perfect. I was poor and I just couldn't get going. It was my first experience of the difference a bad coach can make. The manager was a South African, I can't remember his name, which probably speaks volumes. We would have meetings at his house where he would talk absolute nonsense at us for about three hours. All the players would be bored to tears. Then on the Saturday we would do something entirely different.

Greg was given an old yellow Mini Clubman car and when you went around corners the seat would tip forward and throw you on the floor. Wellington was full of winding roads around the hills and I was for ever being chucked on the floor, much to Greg's amusement. New Zealand, like Newcastle, seemed to be in a time warp. The drinking culture was incredible. Training was once stopped because the players found out that the bar had run out of beer. They refused to carry on until a keg was driven in. They literally wanted to physically see it before they continued. Me and Greg couldn't stop laughing.

The bar at the football club was men only, with a separate lounge for the ladies and this was common in Wellington at this time. Players with families wouldn't even bother going to see them before they started drinking. The whole place was rugby-mad. It didn't matter what time you put on the television or the radio, rugby would be on. One of our favourite moments was when England beat the All Blacks while we were out there. We wouldn't let it drop for weeks. We really pushed the fact that we beat them at a sport they were obsessed about while there was only the north of England and public schoolboys who cared about rugby in England.

We used to fly to some away games in a plane that looked like Biggles used to fly it. It was practically kept together by tape. On one particular turbulent trip the plane was rocking around like a ride at a theme park. You could see out the window as the landscape rose and fell at alarming speeds. Some players were in tears; we really thought we were going to crash. We got to the game about 30 minutes before kick-off. In the warm-up, players were being sick and just falling over. I remember it felt like my legs were still moving even when I was standing still. We were 4-0 down after seven minutes and in the end we lost 4-2.

The social life, however, was something else. The whole team used to go out. At Spurs, I still lived in Welling and so rarely went for a night out with the players, if at all. I used to come home and go out with my friends in Welling instead. In hindsight this was a mistake too as I didn't get some of the shared experiences that the other players had. It is something I would definitely do differently. In Wellington, they had a Maori-run bar that was a bit rough, but it only cost about a tenner to get in and then all your drinks were free. It was mainly Maoris and it could get a bit tasty. We used to go mob-handed in case it ever kicked off. We would spend the first couple of hours playing drinking games so the whole team would be plastered by the end of the night, but we had to be careful not to leave anyone behind. Some of the Maoris were huge and very aggressive.

I used to do a bit of coaching for the club at local schools. It was quite difficult as a lot of children didn't even know what the rules of football were. I had to describe how to score a goal, and that the goalkeeper was the only one who could use their hands. I went into one school and they were having their sports day. The Maori children had to have their own races as otherwise they won everything. It is no wonder the All Blacks were so good at rugby. I saw 11-year-old children who were taller than me and built like heavyweight boxers. You got the impression that there was a lot of tension between the Maori population in Wellington and the other New Zealanders. The Maoris seemed to be treated with a lot of suspicion.

We had a few decent players including our goalkeeper, Frank van Hattum, who had played for New Zealand in the 1982 World Cup against my favourite ever side, the Brazilian team of Éder, Sócrates, Zico and more. Frankie loved the fact that he had let in four goals against that superb side in that World Cup. I was just impressed that he had shared the pitch with my childhood idols. He was practically an old man but was still a decent keeper. We also had a couple of young New Zealanders who had already played for the country's under-23s, but we didn't really do as well as we should have that year and I feel like I let them down. The people at the club behind the scenes were brilliant with me and I don't feel good about how I wasn't honest in the first place. It isn't my proudest moment.

Stuart Prossor, the man whose house I stayed at, was a peculiar man. The house was actually owned by his parents and they lived immediately above him on the side of a hill. I then had my own apartment above them on the same hill. I mean, literally a hill. There were no houses between the three places. I used to have to walk up several hundred steps every night just to get to my room, but I did have an incredible view right over the bay. It was a horseshoe-shaped bay and you could see lots of surfers riding the waves. The airport runway practically touched the sea and you could see the planes coming in and taking off. I would sometimes just sit on the end of my bed and watch the world go by.

Stuart loved football and had written several biographies. He was a keen student of the game and knew a lot. But he was a little weird. We would go out clubbing and invite Stuart along and he would decline, saying he was going to have an early night. We would then see him later in the night wandering around a club by himself. He would try and hide if he saw us, but we had normally already spotted him. He was also a member of a local health club and he would let us come in as his guests. Sometimes, though, we would ask him if he was going to the club and he would say that he wasn't. We would then see his car in the car park of the health club as we drove past. It used to be so infuriating; he only had to say he wanted to go by himself and we wouldn't have minded. In the end we decided to get our own back and stuck a note on his windscreen, saying, 'Hi, I have seen you in the jacuzzi on many occasions but have been too shy to talk. Can you meet me in the bar? I will be the lady with the red top and brown hair.'

We then hid and waited. He went for it hook, line and sinker. He read the note then did his hair in the car window and went inside to the bar. We watched him through the window, sitting there waiting for his mystery woman. Every time someone walked in he would practically jump out his seat to see if it was her. When he came back out, we raced back to the house to get back before him. We had only just sat down when he walked in. Me and Greg were still out of breath and both pretending like we had been watching the television, making silly comments as if we knew what was going on and trying not to laugh. Meanwhile, Stuart was walking up and down the room saying things like, 'very strange' and 'how peculiar', clearly desperate for me or Greg to say something. We didn't take the bait and, in the end, he took great pleasure telling us all about his mystery woman. He even said he thought he knew who it was and told us she was a stunner.

Then Greg, with an Oscar-winning performance, feigned shock that he had left without seeing her. He told Stuart that if it had been him, he would never have left the bar. Within seconds, Stuart was back in his car and returning to the health club. This went on for weeks. Every night he would return. We were happy as it meant he never left us behind and we got into the health club every night. We even got the football club to put an advert in the matchday programme asking for the mystery woman to come forward. I don't remember if Stuart ever found out. If not, please accept my belated apology.

The regular season in New Zealand started in March and finished after the season starts in England, running for about 18 games. I can honestly say that I wasn't match-fit until about our 14th fixture. As I said before, I felt very guilty about letting down the club, especially as I knew I had gone out there on false pretences. After the regular fixtures are finished, teams in the top half play in one cup competition while the lower-half teams play in another. We were one point short of making the top half and I didn't fancy playing in the wooden spoon tournament. These cups start at about the same time teams in England return for pre-season training. I was now 22 and was starting to consider a career away from football, but I decided to leave New Zealand early and have one more go at it. This meant I had to pay for my own flight, but I didn't care, I was ready to go home. As much as I enjoyed my time, I was starting to get a little homesick. My sister got married while I was in New Zealand, and not being there was tough.

I started the 1994/95 season at Erith & Belvedere, who had a lot of investment behind them. The manager was Harry Richardson and his coach was Nicky Brigden. Because of the money we had a decent side and Sean Devine, who I had played with at Phoenix, was our best player. He was a completely different player to the one I had left behind at Phoenix. He now worked in a gym which he used every day, and he had a real work ethic. He was a bit like a Jamie Vardy – always on the move and he had pace to burn. Sean was only there for 12 games before moving on to bigger and better things, and in that time he scored a stack of goals He was ready to take the next step and went on to enjoy a long professional career.

Nicky Brigden was an excellent coach, and had already had great success as a manager with Welling United at the highest level of non-league football. On a much smaller budget than every other team he had consistently got Welling into the top ten and had also overseen some great runs in the FA Cup. He had studied the Wimbledon style of football, getting it down to a fine art, and his teams were very well regimented. If you have got this far into my book and you know anything about football you will know that this approach did not appeal to me or suit my style of play. I had a lot of respect for Nicky, who knew I had talent and desperately tried to find a place for me, but he was intelligent enough to know I didn't fit in.

Harry Richardson was something else altogether! He was a large man in both personality and stature. He was a good judge of player and knew everyone in non-league football, but seemed to base his prowess as a manger on the fact that he had survived four Crown Court cases. Then there were the team talks. First there would be Nicky, who was succinct and to the point. His talks were excellent and we would be very aware of everyone's jobs on the pitch. Then Harry would start, and he would be just noise. They were hugely entertaining but lacked any content. For example, a couple of months into the season we were playing away to Tonbridge Angels, one of our local rivals. We were all changed and in the dressing room about ten minutes before kick-off. I was a substitute as I was on my way back from another twisted ankle. Nicky had just finished his part of the talk when Harry stepped up. Well, it was the most over-the-top, funny rant I had ever heard. He started slowly but, as these things tend to, it built up to a crescendo. At first, he spoke about how much he hated Tonbridge. The fact they were out in the Kent countryside seemed to be the main issue he had with them, with lots of farmer references being used, but the end was incredible. By now he was shouting and I can't remember the whole of it but some parts will be for ever burnt on my mind and it went something like, 'Treat this lot like Cozzers and grasses, slit their throats while they sleep, take no prisoners. Leave them bleeding in their beds!'

For those not familiar with 'Sarf Londonese', Cozzers are the police. I genuinely wanted to laugh out loud, but when I looked around everyone had clearly bought into it. We went out on to that pitch like the British Army going over the top at the Somme into no-man's land, and within 20 minutes we were down to nine men! Sean Devine was one of the players sent off. Sean's new-found attitude had meant that he was already intense on the pitch, and thanks to Harry's team talk he was out of control. After he was sent off for trying to fight their centre-half, he literally jumped into the crowd to try and fight a fan who was shouting abuse at him.

At half-time we were two goals and two players down. Normally I would have stayed on the pitch and kicked a ball about in case I was needed, but I had to see what Harry was going to say. His comments were interesting:

'I don't believe you lot! We come down here for a friendly game of football and look what happens.'

I had to leave the room to stop myself from laughing.

But this was part of the problem; I couldn't take the football seriously. I used to sit in the changing room seeing everyone so wound up and into the game and I would feel guilty. I didn't really care if we won or lost. I didn't want to be there and wanted to be back at Spurs, but I knew that couldn't happen. I have since spoken to a lot of people who had similar experiences. When you start at that level, it is very difficult to get yourself motivated to play lower down. It got so bad that I even tried hypnosis. Nothing worked. I was lost.

My ankles were still not right either. I would get to the night for training and not want to go. That had never happened before. I would even be relieved if matches were called off. There was a lot of travelling in that league and sometimes I would leave my house at nine in the morning and get back at ten at night. I hated it. In the end, Nicky Brigden found the perfect position for me on the team: substitute. I didn't fit into the team the way they played, but if things were going wrong then they would throw me on and hope I could pull a rabbit out of the hat. When I started, I would be a passenger, just watching the ball going backwards and forwards over my head. Nicky was exactly right starting me from the bench; I would have done the same thing too. It was still strange, though, as every week I was the best player in training and then the game would come and I would be on the bench.

Then, in early 1995, it was a freezing cold night and we were driving to some hole in the middle of nowhere to play a game that I didn't even want to be a part of. It was raining, and there was a huge part of me that hoped the match would be called off so I could just go back home. By then, in the build-up I wouldn't know whether my ankle would be okay or not. I would be walking on it and testing it out all week. On the day of the game I would have a few practice jogs, but I wouldn't be sure that I would be okay to play until I went out for the warm-up. It was no way to prepare. I was sitting on the coach looking out of the window when, on the radio, they announced the England squad for a game being played the following week. Ian Walker, Nick Barmby and Jamie Redknapp were all named, and Paul Gascoigne was also back in. As I stared at the rain hitting the window, I remember just laughing out loud. It was so awful it was funny. One of the other players asked me what was funny. I told him that I just realised I had done my career in reverse.

The next day I enrolled for teacher training and my football dream was officially over. I was 23 years old.

Epilogue

I TELL myself that I have no real regrets. What doesn't kill you makes you stronger and all that. It's true that I *am* a happy person with a life and a family I love. I had an awful experience in my first marriage, that could be a book on its own, or maybe a *Jeremy Kyle* episode at least. I am thankful for meeting my second wife, Sonya, and look forward to my life ahead. I gave up on football a long time ago. I still played, but a version far from the one I played previously.

This book was about my dream. It was about the lack of support for young, vulnerable men at the most difficult periods of their lives. I followed my dream as far as I could physically take it. In the end, it was my childhood that caught up with me. The concrete halls, concrete AstroTurf and awful pitches. Too much too young. In truth, my career was already over before it began.

In a book about dreams, it is fitting that only in my dreams do I truly show myself. Nearly every dream I wake up and remember is a variation of the one that has gone before. I have earned a trial. It is always set in the present time, no matter what my age. At the trial, the other players are always from my time at Spurs, frozen in time as my memory remembers them. In my head I know I belong; it is right that I am there. This is my chance to show that I *do* belong. In the dream, there is always something that stops me taking part in the trial. I can't find the venue or I have lost my kit, or sometimes I just can't physically move and never seem to get closer. I have never yet made it to the trial, not in nearly 30 years of trying. Perhaps in a lifetime of trying.

People tell me that I should feel lucky because I made it. I was a professional footballer in the Premier League. But this wasn't the making it that I dreamed of. In my dreams as a kid, I never walked away into the sunset without anyone noticing.

Also available at all good book stores

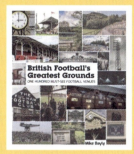

9781785316470

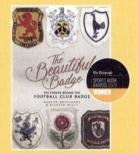

9781785313929

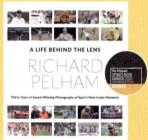

9781785315466

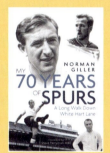

9781785318894

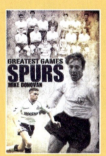

9781908051776

9781785313264

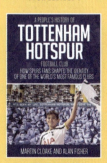

9781785311888

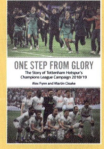

9781785315985

9781905411863